SIR GAWAIN AND THE GREEN KNIGHT

NOTES

With notes on *Pearl* and brief commentary on *Purity* and *Patience*.

including
- *A Note on the Text*
- *A Note on Interpretation and the Use of This Volume*
- *Introduction*
- *Language and Style*
- *Summaries and Commentaries*
- *Review Questions*
- *Selected Bibliography*

by
John Gardner, Ph.D.
Department of English
Southern Illinois University

WILEY

Wiley Publishing, Inc.

Editor
Gary Carey, M.A., University of Colorado

Consulting Editor
James L. Roberts, Ph.D., Department of
English, University of Nebraska

Publisher's Acknowledgments
Senior Project Editor: Michael Kelly
Acquisitions Editor: Greg Tubach
Glossary Editors: The editors and staff at
Webster's New World Dictionaries
Editorial Administrator: Michelle Hacker
Editorial Assistant: Brian Herrmann

Composition
Wiley Indianapolis Composition Services

CliffsNotes™ *Sir Gawain and the Green Knight*

Published by:
Wiley Publishing, Inc.
111 River Street
Hoboken, NJ 07030
www.wiley.com

Copyright © 2001 Wiley Publishing, Inc., Hoboken, New Jersey
ISBN: 0-8220-0515-8

10 9 8 7 6
1MA/RV/QU/QW/IN
Published by Wiley Publishing, Inc., Hoboken, New Jersey
Published simultaneously in Canada

CONTENTS

A Note on the Text

The work of the Gawain- or Pearl-poet survives in a single manuscript, the Cotton Nero A.x., named for the bust under which it once stood in the Cotton library, now in the British Museum. The manuscript contains four poems, *Pearl, Purity* (or *Cleanness*), *Patience,* and *Sir Gawain and the Green Knight.* Similarities of style, dialect, and theme strongly suggest that the four poems are all the work of a single writer. A fifth poem, *St. Erkenwald,* not found in the same manuscript, has sometimes been attributed to the same poet but is almost certainly the work of another hand.

For a list of the various editions of the poems, both in the original Middle English and in modernized versions, see the Selected Bibliography. The basis of the present volume of Notes is the modernized version by John Gardner, *The Complete Works of the Gawain-Poet,* but where the modernization sharply departs from the original text the editions followed are *Pearl,* ed. E. V. Gordon; *Sir Gawain and the Green Knight,* ed. Sir Israel Gollancz; and, occasionally, *Pearl and Sir Gawain and the Green Knight,* ed. A. C. Cawley.

A Note on Interpretation and the Use of This Volume

There is considerable disagreement at present on how medieval literature ought to be understood, and it is impossible within the limits of this volume to give equal space to all points of view. These Notes present close paraphrase of *Pearl* and *Sir Gawain* with brief summaries of the less well known *Purity* and *Patience,* in order that the student may see the apparent continuity of the whole Cotton Nero A.x., both in theme and in technique. Summaries and commentary are presented together, and the commentary is aimed mainly at making the poet's more obvious meanings and devices apparent. For more elaborate readings of the poems, see the Selected Bibliography.

But even the conservative readings offered here may not meet with approval from every scholar and teacher. The reader should therefore bear in mind that alternative views are available. One is that the poems cannot be read together because they may not be the work of the same man (at present, the point cannot be proved one way or the other). If it is separated from the rest of the poems, *Sir Gawain and the Green Knight* can easily be read as a poem built of ancient pagan rituals; it is, in other words, a vegetation myth with a thin overlay of Christian sermonizing—or at any rate, that argument has been presented. Some details in the poem do not work by this reading, but the assumption is that we should not expect them to: the poem is in effect a primitive work, not meant to be fully controlled.

Another point of view is that *Sir Gawain* cannot be understood except by reference to earlier romance tradition. In other romances Gawain is treacherous and lecherous; remembering this, it has been argued, we see that the Gawain of the poem is not what he appears: he is pretending to others and himself that he is an innocent, but actually he is a man whose reputation is not good (despite what other characters in the poem say), but bad. This approach, taken by Professor Larry Benson in a recent book, results in an ingenious and fascinating reading; but it assumes the poet's use of a tradition we cannot be sure he accepted or even knew as well as we do. In his own part of England, at all events, other poets before and after him treated Gawain as the very emblem of virtue, not treacherous and lecherous like the Gawain of French romances.

Still another reading finds all of *Sir Gawain* a strict religious allegory, every piece of armor, every tree, every trinket or curl a subtle emblem drawn out of scripture or the writings of the church fathers. This reading has the advantage of making the poem fit very nicely with the explicitly religious poems preceding it in the manuscript, but it narrows the poem considerably, leaves numerous details unexplained, and assigns arbitrary values to details which seem to have different values in the flow of drama. For instance, if the armor of Gawain all refers to "the whole armor of God," then the symbolism is very queer.

Gawain's arming, described in detail, recalls the description of the unarmed Green Knight (he comes in clothes he calls "soft"): he carries—and needs—no defensive arms, only the huge weapon of offense, his ax. Gawain, on the other hand, who is forbidden to defend himself from the Green Knight's blow, has elaborate though useless defensive trappings, the description of which culminates in the image of the shield, parallel to the image of the ax. Civilization has given poor Gawain everything he could possibly need in any battle but the one he has undertaken. The thoroughly religious reading of the poem may also have some trouble accounting for the poet's humor throughout.

Other readings focus on timeless qualities of the poems: on their interest as psychological studies, their delight in contrasting reality and merely human verbal systems of reality, and so forth. Such readings are valuable and often legitimate, but they are too private to be offered in these Notes.

The Notes presented here, in short, are designed to help the student and teacher focus on the texts themselves, to notice difficulties and points of interest that might otherwise slip by, and to notice solutions to some difficulties in the texts. The Notes borrow those insights from other critics or critical schools which seem to clarify the poem, and they silently pass over opinions that seem to raise more questions than they answer. The student interested in using these Notes well will think through the reading offered here and will make it merely the starting point for his own thoughtful reading of the poems and study of the criticism.

Introduction

Each of the four poems commonly ascribed to the Gawain-poet is a masterpiece of its own kind. The first poem in the group, *Pearl*, ranks among the best elegies in English, and the last, *Sir Gawain and the Green Knight*, is commonly described as the greatest Arthurian romance in our literary tradition. The two middle poems, *Purity* and *Patience*, are superb examples of a genre no longer highly favored but much admired throughout the Middle Ages, the so-called verse homily or religious meditation. Among English poets of the later Middle Ages, the Gawain-poet is often said to stand second only to Chaucer.

Nothing is known about the Gawain-poet's life. He wrote in the dialect of the northwest Midlands of fourteenth-century England, and he may have lived most or all of his life in Yorkshire or Lancashire. He may have served in one of the provincial courts, since there is ample evidence in his poetry that he knew aristocratic activities. He makes easy and comfortable use of the technical language of hunting, hawking, cooking, chess, and the like; he knew the special language of the lawyer, furrier, architect, courtly lover, and priest; he was extremely familiar with the Bible and with biblical commentary, probably even commentary in Hebrew.

The imagery which has greatest immediacy in all his poems is imagery of the country: fields, barns, rivers, cliffs, forests, villages, wild animals, birds, seasonal changes. But the poet's use of this imagery is shot through with intellectual subtlety. Sometimes this subtlety lies in his use of concrete images to express abstract or mystical ideas. For instance, in *Pearl* he compares man's struggle against the will of God with the struggle of a trapped deer:

Be now
Less proud, for though you dance like a doe

And brandish and bray with all your rage,
When you make no headway to or fro,
Then you'll abide what He will judge.

At other times he uses concrete images emblematically, that is, as signs of abstract concepts. *Sir Gawain and the Green Knight* provides numerous examples of this, the most striking of which is the poet's apparent use of a deer hunt, a boar hunt, and a fox hunt as emblematic representations of three tests of the qualities of Sir Gawain's soul. (See the discussion of the poem, below.)

On other occasions the poet uses images in a still more complex allegorical fashion, drawing upon — and elaborating on — traditional allegorical readings of biblical images. For example, the whale which swallows Jonah in *Patience* is identified in the poem, as in the writings of the early church fathers, with hell. The poet does not limit himself to allegory which is traditional, however; he frequently invents new allegorical devices.

Finally, he uses concrete images in a way which can only be described as symbolic. Sir Gawain's shield, with its image of the pentangle on the outside, the Virgin Mary on the inside, is emblematic of Gawain's virtues, but it does not function simply as an emblem (the concrete representation of an abstract concept); both in itself and in Gawain's way of using it, it brings a variety of ideas and actions into focus. It symbolizes the chivalric life, calls attention to the conflict, central to the poem, between Christian and courtly love, and ironically comments on Gawain's mistaken acceptance of a wrong kind of "shield," the belt whose magic will, he hopes, save his life when he encounters the dangerous green man.

The poet's considerable knowledge of courtly and scholarly things, his intellectual bent, and his characteristic concerns with religion, law, and courtly love have led to numerous speculations about his identity. One suggestion, not generally accepted but by no means impossible, is that he was a priest, perhaps a private chaplain to a nobleman. All of the poems except *Sir Gawain* are explicitly religious and show a general knowledge of exegetical typology and Christian philosophy, and even *Sir Gawain* explores a religious theme.

The fact that the poet had a child (the daughter lamented in *Pearl)* need not work against this theory, for as Professor C. G. Coulton argued, the poet may have entered the priesthood after the death of his wife, who may conceivably have been dead already at the time he composed *Pearl.* No wife is mentioned in the poem, and the poet speaks of grieving all alone. On the other hand, if he was a priest he must not have become one until after the composition of *Pearl,* where he speaks of "God whom, in the form of bread and wine,/ The priest reveals to us every day." This does not sound like the speech of a man who is himself a priest, and it places us in the awkward position of excluding the poet's greatest religious poem from our explanation of why he wrote religious poems.

Another suggestion sometimes advanced is that the poet may have been a lawyer, possibly Chaucer's neighbor "philosophical Strode," Thomist philosopher at Merton College, later well known London lawyer. The argument for Strode is weak, but it is by no means impossible that the poet was, like many young men destined for service in major or minor courts, trained in law. At all events, it is very likely indeed that the poet did do service of some kind in a court. Given his fondness for speaking both literally and allegorically, it seems possible that he means both God and some actual feudal lord when he writes, in the prologue to *Patience:*

> For lo, if my liege lord likes, in this life, to command me
> Either to ride or to run or to roam on his errand,
> What good is my grumbling except to get greater griefs?
> And if he commands me to talk, though my tongue be raw,
> I must do what his power impels, despite displeasure,
> And bow myself to his bidding, be worthy my hire.

But aside from speculations of this kind, we can say nothing about the poet. No one of his time mentioned him by name, and no relevant records have been discovered.

As for the poems, they are a product of the so-called alliter-ative renaissance. This term may be misleading and has been much debated, but it is probably legitimate within limits. It was once a common scholarly opinion that fourteenth-century English poets, particularly poets of the west Midlands, con-sciously revived the dead or virtually dead tradition of alliterative poetry which went back to Anglo-Saxon times. Scholars today are less sure that the old tradition stood in need of revival: it may have come down in an unbroken chain to the fourteenth century. They argue that the absence of transitional manuscripts proves nothing, since we know that nearly everything from the period of transition has been lost; and they point to suggestions in Middle English alliterative poems that the tradition did survive. The clearest suggestion is the poet's statement in *Sir Gawain and the Green Knight* that he intends to tell his story

> Rightly, as it is written,
> A story swift and strong
> With letters locked and linking,
> As scops have always sung.

(Literally, the last line reads, "As long has been in the land.") But it is not true that the poet is telling an old, well known story or one that he heard, as he tells us elsewhere, "in town," and there is no real indication in these lines that the "locked and linking" alliterative form came down to the poet as a vital poetic method rather than as a dimly remembered antique.

In any case, as Professor Larry Benson has recently argued most convincingly, to fourteenth-century English poets the appeal of alliterative verse was probably not its long tradition but its usefulness as a mode of elevated rhetoric. The rhetorical devices which had recently come into fashion in England were beautifully suited to the alliterative style, and it may have been this that prompted poets to revive, or at least adopt, the ancient poetic method. (For more detailed comment on the alliterative method, see Language and Style, below.)

The chief interest of the works of the Gawain-poet is not, however, that they reflect a curious fourteenth-century fashion.

They are vastly superior to all other poems in the same general style—*Piers Plowman,* the alliterative *Morte Arthure, Winner and Waster,* and *The Parliament of the Three Ages.*

The Gawain-poet's work abounds with sharply defined images, powerfully conceived scenes, richly sensuous details— colors, scents, textures. He is a master of suspense, irony, humor. His castles are the noblest, most dazzling in English poetry; his gloomy woods are the gloomiest; his ladies are the most alluring.

In addition to all this, his poetry is the most ornamental successful poetry in English. In *Pearl,* lines both alliterate and rhyme, and verbal echoes link the stanzas. In all his poems he echoes his opening lines in his closing lines; and his alliteration within individual lines or groups of lines is ingenious.

His organization of each poem is remarkably complex, yet flawless, scene balanced against scene, image balanced against image. And a careful reading of the group of poems suggests that the whole Cotton Nero A.x. manuscript, the "Pearl group," as I will call it, is yet another ingeniously organized system. The poems are both independent pieces and parts of a meaningful whole.

The poet's interest in ornamentation and schematic elabora- tion is not unique in the fourteenth century. On the contrary, nothing is more common. One finds it in Chaucer's neat juxta- position of three disparate love stories in the *Book of the Duchess* (if we accept the standard interpretation) or in Chaucer's bal- ancing of contrasting points of view in *The Canterbury Tales;* one finds it in the English mystery plays, in riddles and puzzle lyrics, and so on. The same delight in ornamentation and in- genious schemata appears in medieval music, painting, architec- ture, and religion.

The Gawain-poet did not invent his method but carried the esthetic fashion of his day to its logical extremity. (His Scottish imitators in the next generation carried technical ingenuity further yet, introducing still more difficult systems of rhyme and alliteration, verbal linking, and so on; but to do so they had to sacrifice characterization, drama, and atmosphere—a price too high to pay for surface glitter.)

And the Gawain-poet differs from some of his contemporaries in that his use of ornamental devices is never merely ornamental. Take *Pearl*, for example. Sir Israel Gollancz pointed out long ago that the twelve-line stanzas of *Pearl* should probably be viewed as imitations of the primitive twelve-line Italian sonnet. The linked ring of one hundred and one sonnets or stanzas in *Pearl* is symbolically related to the transmutation within the poem of flower imagery into jeweled-flower imagery (Nature into Art), reflecting the contrast between mortal life and eternal life. The circular poem becomes itself an emblem of the "garland" of the blessed—a circle of artificial flowers—around the throne of God. In the hundred-and-first stanza the circle, or cycle, begins again: the human narrator's pursuit of perfect happiness has not been finally successful; he too must begin again.

Compare the time scheme in *Sir Gawain*, a year and a day. In both poems, of course, the idea that confession makes possible a new beginning, is central and explicit.

For the reader not yet thoroughly familiar with medieval literature and habits of thought, the works of the Gawain-poet are likely to be difficult, for much that medieval poets took for granted is relatively foreign to our present way of thinking. For one thing, medieval poetry is highly conventional in the sense that it returns again and again to a few central images, themes, and techniques. Whereas the modern poet prides himself on describing what is unique and personal, medieval poets characteristically chose old and much worked images and prided themselves on subtly modifying them to make them fit as if naturally and inevitably into a new context.

The image of the love garden or earthly paradise, for example, is one found in hundreds of medieval poems, from the pious to the bawdy. The image has a stock set of associations—

with Eden, with heaven, with the transience of life (flowers wither all too quickly), with overweening pride, and so forth. This image is one which appears in all of Chaucer's dream-visions, in *Troilus,* in many of the *Canterbury Tales,* and in the *Legend of Good Women,* and it is treated each time in a new way.

The Gawain-poet is equally adept at ringing changes on a traditional image. *Pearl* opens in a garden of sorts—it has the conventional herbs and colors—but this time the garden is a graveyard, the season is not May but August, the time of harvest, and the conventional association of the garden with love is queerly twisted. The narrator of the poem is indeed reciting a love-complaint of sorts, and he does speak of himself, metaphorically, as a courtly lover. He describes himself as "fordolked of luf-daungere," that is, robbed of his lover's right; but he has been robbed not by a human rival but by Christ, who, in medieval scriptural typology, is the bridegroom of every soul.

The sorrowful garden in which *Pearl* opens looks forward to the true garden of Paradise, where the narrator finds himself in his dream; and it also looks forward to the vineyard of Christ's parable, introduced into the poem, a vineyard emblematic of the universal church. Every detail in the poet's description of the graveyard-garden where the narrator falls asleep is picked up and turned to new significance in the later gardens.

The same conventional garden image is picked up again, and again treated in a new way, in the second poem in the Pearl group, *Purity.* Sodom and the rest of the wicked cities seem to be heaven on earth, gardens more beautiful than Eden, to their inhabitants; but they prove to be false paradises. Where they sink into the earth there comes to be a terrible sea (the Dead Sea) emblematic of hell. If a man is pushed into that sea by murderers he suffers torments but cannot die until the end of time; and around the shore grow seemingly beautiful trees,

Oranges, pomegranates, and other things,
And all so red and ripe and richly hued
That one might well believe them sweet indeed;

But when that fruit is broken or bitten in two,
It reveals not the beauty of earth but blowing ashes.

In later sections of *Purity,* and in *Patience* as well, the poet rings
further changes on the convention. In *Sir Gawain and the Green
Knight,* the traditional image of the bountiful garden of love is
one of many things coloring Gawain's experience at Hautdesert
Castle.

The poet makes ingenious use of many stock images of this
kind, and one of the most fruitful ways of approaching his poetry,
at least for the specialist in medieval literature and culture, is to
examine each of his images closely in the light of its tradition.
One finds that the castle Sir Gawain discovers in the forest has
rich medieval associations: it is like a phantom castle — the lovely
white castles constructed by Morgan le Fay's magic as castles of
temptation; it is like the traditional temple of love in some
respects; and it is like the stock medieval image of heaven
(found in *Pearl,* for example).

One finds that the Green Knight, one of the most strikingly
original creations in all English literature, is the result of an
equally brilliant manipulation of traditional materials. Primarily
he is a "blurred" combination of two stock figures, the traditional elf (a dignified and beautiful natural creature, man-like but
in many ways superior to man, in the medieval view) and the
traditional "wild man," a dangerous, irrational, slightly sub-
human creature. The sense of mystery that surrounds the Green
Knight has its main source in this blending together of irrecon-
cilable myth figures. (For full discussion of the two traditions
and the poet's blending of them, see Larry Benson's *Art and
Tradition in Sir Gawain and the Green Knight,* pp. 58 ff.)

But the poet has further enriched his creation by drawing on
other traditions as well. The medieval Devil also wears green,
comes from the mysterious north, and tests men's souls. Cupid,
in the Middle Ages, was a famous hunter, both of animals and
of the human heart. And the Druid magicians of British tradition
were, like the Green Knight, shape-shifters associated with oak
woods and barrows.

Needless to say, the beginning reader of medieval literature annot see the details in any given poem in the light of all nedieval literary tradition, and there is no need that he do so. It is enough to know that the poem's details are largely the products of a long tradition of subtle manipulation of a few stock elements. Knowing this, one can watch for clues within the poem or group of poems, and one can guess out for oneself the poet's meaning.

In the Pearl group one can notice, for instance, that the New Jerusalem at the end of *Pearl* is described as a city in walls, or castle, and that great emphasis is given to the number *twelve*. One can then notice that in *Purity* another castle, clearly a far cry from holy, is described in terms which recall the description of the New Jerusalem, and that emphasis is given to the number *seven*. One can notice that the city to which Jonah comes in *Patience* faintly recalls city descriptions in *Pearl* and *Purity,* and that the description of Camelot in *Sir Gawain and the Green Knight* clearly and emphatically echoes the description of Belshazzar's sinful castle and its revels; and Hautdesert Castle similarly recalls Belshazzar's.

If one understands that medieval poets often prided themselves on developing, in a new and unique way, firmly established "topics" or conventions, one should have no trouble in identifying the castle image as one of the topics; and observing the contrast between the heavenly castle in *Pearl* and Belshazzar's castle in *Purity,* one should have no difficulty in discovering that the order represented by any image of a castle may be a true order or a false one.

If one suspects that the *twelves* and *sevens* of the contrasting descriptions may be symbolic, one can easily check any dictionary of symbolism or numerology (in which case one will find that *twelve* is emblematic of the risen church, the New City which was adumbrated in the twelve tribes of the earthly Israel and was founded by the twelve apostles; *seven* is the number of the mortal — four elements (fire, air, water, earth) and three kinds of soul (rational, irascible, concupiscent) — in other words the number of the merely human).

One of the comforting things about medieval literature is that much of its symbolism—though by no means all of it—is standard enough to be available in symbol dictionaries. The reader must of course be careful in identifying symbols: the same thing may have opposite meanings, depending on its context—for instance, a lion may represent either Christ or Satan, depending on the passage in which it occurs, and in other passages it can mean other things, the idea of kingship, or the rational faculty in man, or something else. (If all this seems difficult, compare the symbolism of nineteenth- and early twentieth-century French poets.)

In the works of the Gawain-poet, as in the poetry of Chaucer, one can get a fairly good understanding of what is going on merely by reading closely, making occasional guesses, and checking dictionaries to see if the guess can be supported. The emphasis here should of course be on the close reading. In medieval poetry, just as in scripture as medieval people understood it, nothing is obscurely hinted in one place that is not made clear in another.

To put all this another way, the best way for the beginner to approach allegory and symbolism in medieval poetry may be to make sure he understands its *method,* because a knowledge of the method makes it possible for the reader to guess out the meaning of particular allegorical or symbolic details.

Reduced to essentials, the method works this way. Everything that exists in the world is an expression of God's nature or some aspect of God's nature; in other words, the universe is a "vast array of emblems," or "the world is the language of God." Thus Adam, looking at gold, could presumably see that part of God's nature was beauty; looking at a fawn he could see other attributes of God. Before the fall, man could look at Nature and understand God and God's will for man directly; but after the fall man's wits became dim and he needed what St. Bonaventura calls a second, clearer book—scripture. To dim-witted, fallen man, gold seemed beautiful in itself, not in its meaning, and God's will became difficult to separate from baser human desires.

Because of the way the Holy Ghost composes, in the medieval view, scripture reveals truth in a number of ways. Sometimes it tells the truth directly, in which case we say it is "literal," and sometimes it tells it indirectly, in which case it speaks in an allegorical fashion, and sometimes it speaks in both ways at once. For instance, the story of Joshua at the walls of Jericho is both a literal story, a true historical report, on one hand, and, on the other, an allegorical allusion to the Last Judgment, in which all the walls of the world will be overthrown by Gabriel's horn.

Examined carefully, according to the patristic exegetes (the church fathers who interpreted scripture), Old Testament events foreshadow New Testament events. Moses striking a rock and releasing water to quench the thirst of the Children of Israel in the wilderness foreshadows the striking of Christ (the Rock), whose flowing blood and water will save the spiritual Children of Israel, that is, Christians. Again, Noah, who saves the only good men of his time — his family — by floating them to safety on an ark, foreshadows Christ, who will float Christians to safety in his church.

Many Old Testament figures are interpreted in this allegorical fashion, among them Adam, Abel, Isaac, Joseph, Samson. Some foreshadow Christ because they are like him in some respect, for example Job, who, like Christ, is infinitely patient; some suggest Christ because they are antithetical (they are "antitypes"), for example Jonah, who, unlike Christ, is impatient. And of course not all Old Testament figures look forward to Christ. Eve looks forward to her antitype, the Virgin; Cain and Nimrod (according to tradition the builder of the Tower of Babel) suggested the Devil. Certain women are allegorical representatives of the church, Christ's bride. (Cf. the conclusion of *Pearl.)*

This allegorical way of looking at things applies not only to Old Testament events but to daily life and to pagan literature as well. If the events in the Old Testament are the language of God, then all events must be; and even a literary work which may not have been directly inspired by the Holy Ghost may nevertheless carry mystical meaning. Thus Vergil's *Aeneid* was commonly interpreted as an allegory of the soul's flight to the New Jerusalem or, on another level, as Christ's foundation of the heavenly city.

From this point of view, pagan gods are obviously mis-apprehensions of true divinity. Thus Cupid may be, as he is in Chaucer's *Troilus and Criseyde*, both a false god and an adum-bration, or imperfect apprehension, of the true God of Love, Christ. In turn, Cupid's garden and Cupid's hunting may be viewed as allegorical suggestions of the earthly paradise, where Adam's love for God gave way to cupidinous love, in other words, love for a woman—a hunt by the Devil for Adam's heart; or, on the other hand, Cupid's garden may be viewed as an allegory of the heavenly garden, paradise, and the hunt may represent God's hunt for the heart of man.

All this is not as confusing as it seems. The point, very simply, is that the stock *topics* of medieval poetry are not fixed in their meaning. They are fixed, simply, as topics. The fixed conventional images and events may be pure representations of holy reality, but they can as easily be made pure representations of devilish illusion, that is, the Devil's counterfeit of the holy; and they can also be—as they usually are—ambiguous things which can be read in either of two ways, rightly (worshipfully) or wrongly (sinfully). A beautiful woman may be a symbol of God's love or may be a sex object. The symbol in question may derive from scripture, from pagan literature, from folklore, or from everyday life.

As for treatment, it may be presented in such a way that it is unmistakably a symbol (cf. Gawain's shield, on which the poet comments at considerable length in explication of the allegorical meaning), or it may be presented in intensely realistic terms so that we recognize only afterward that the detail was allegorical. Thus, for example, the temptation scenes in Gawain's bedroom are treated with comic realism: they seem merely a sexual struggle between an almost excessively genteel knight and a beautiful country girl with no inhibitions; we discover later that what was involved was not simple sexual play but shrewd and sophisticated temptation.

But this discussion of the medieval symbolic method leaves out one crucial consideration. The concern of art, even the least realistic art, is never with "what ought to be," in Sidney's phrase, but with the tension between what ought to be and what *can* be. It is one thing to declare in an abstract treatise in theology or philosophy, "Renounce the world" or "Love only God." It is another to say such things to a medieval knight.

A knight is a man charged with the responsibility of preserving order in the world; his fighting equipment is shockingly expensive for two reasons, both strictly practical: first, it takes an artist to temper a sword perfectly, to make armor both impenetrable and light, and both the artist and his equipment (raw materials and tools) are expensive by the law of supply and demand; second, a knight's accouterments have psychological as well as kinematic effect: the greater the fighter, the more elegant his gear, because a knight who is well paid and has often taken booty can afford a jeweled helmet like Gawain's, a scarlet cape, an ermine collar, and the rest; coming up against such a knight, a man does well to surrender on the spot.

Now the problem is, how is a knight to understand the prescription "Renounce the world"? Ideally, of course, he maintains an attitude of pious indifference to the worldly power and glory he emblematically represents. But the ideal is virtually impossible to achieve. As for the prescription "Love only God," it stands in tacit conflict with the ancient and venerable doctrine embodied in the whole system of courtly love: a man gets heart on the battlefield by thinking of the loved ones he is there to protect – in Anglo-Saxon times, the friends and relatives of his meadhall, in the later Middle Ages, the lady he is sworn to serve.

Ideally, of course, the knight should love some pale ideal of womanhood, for example the Virgin, whom Gawain serves. But again the ideal is hard to live by when the competition is strong.

In short, a wise medieval poet does not contrast simple good and evil, in other words, simple righteousness versus sinfulness. He tests ideals against the possible.

We see the same sort of testing in *Pearl,* and again the same two questions are central: How is one to renounce the world? and How can one love only God? In this poem the narrator would like nothing better than to renounce the world and join his dead child in heaven; but his attempt to do so, at the end of the poem, is rebuffed. He would like nothing better than to love God, if it meant he could be with his dead daughter; but it is not easy to love the God who has robbed you of your child, leaving you solitary.

The Gawain-poet does not pretend to solve these dilemmas. He dramatizes them, accepts the orthodox solutions, and tries to live by them without pretending to himself that they are fully satisfactory. There are no satisfactory solutions to the human situation; there are merely ways of getting up again when you're down. Not, of course, that the Gawain-poet blames the God who is man's enemy and friend. Accepting the miserable condition of fallen man, accepting responsibility for it, he struggles to find what will serve.

What serves, in the Pearl group, is two great medieval doctrines, purity and patience. Through purity one is lifted directly to heaven: this is the way of innocents, that is, children and saints. Through patience one works one's way to heaven. One patiently accepts one's subservient position and serves God as loyally as one can. If one slips, one repents and starts over. In the first poem in the group, *Pearl,* the child reached heaven by purity; the narrator must reach heaven by patience. In the second and third poems, *Purity* and *Patience,* the two ideas are explored in a biblical context and are, in each poem, systematically contrasted with one another. In the concluding poem, *Sir Gawain,* a knight famous for his purity fails a test in the wilderness and must now learn Christian patience.

All this is not to say that the interest in the poems is simply and strictly religious. Medieval religion is one way in which human beings have struggled to deal with problems shared by religious and unreligious men and cultures. The greatness of the poems lies in their accurate representation of human feelings and the universal process of life, whatever metaphysic we may call upon to explain it all or to make the unhappiness easier to bear, the joy more permanent. The poet's vision has as much to do with the contrast between civilization and wilderness, winter and summer, as with heaven and earth. And his poems are — above all, perhaps — a powerful and vivid record of how it felt to live in fourteenth-century England.

Language and Style

The language of the original poems is the fourteenth-century northwest Midlands dialect of Middle English, a dialect like Chaucer's in many respects but different in sound (consonants are sharper, vowels more open, generally), different in some of its common forms ("ho" for Chaucer's "she"), more heavily influenced by Scandinavian vocabulary, and in some ways closer to Old English. The poet's language had a rich tradition of alliterative formulas ("the *t*rammels of *t*reason," i.e., in the original, "þe trammes of tresoun"). (For discussion of linguistic and phonological features of the northwest Midlands dialect, see the Selected Bibliography.)

What is chiefly of interest for our present purpose is the poet's manner of handling the language of his time and place. For one thing, he employs a remarkably large vocabulary which gives vitality and richness to his lines. (Compare, in this respect, the quality of Wallace Stevens' verse, with its many borrowings from French, German, and other languages, its delight in rare words juxtaposed to common words—"In kitchen cups concupiscent curds"—and so forth.)

Stylistic studies of his verse, the most recent of which is Miss Borroff's (see Selected Bibliography), show that the poet delighted in slightly altering traditional alliterative formulas for ironic effect. For example, the old formula "stiff in stead," meaning "courageous or stalwart in his battle-place," becomes, in *Sir Gawain and the Green Knight*, "stiff in stall," that is, "stalwart in his chair at the dinner table." The poet's playful approach to language shows up in other ways as well. In *Sir Gawain* we find the lines,

Hit watȝ Ennias þe athel & his highe kynde
þat siþen depreced prouinces, & patrounes bicome
Welneȝe of al þe wele in þe west iles,

Fro riche Romulus to Rome ricchis hym swyþe;
With gret bobbaunce þat burȝe he biges vpon fyrst....
(GGK, 5-9)

in modern English,

> Aeneas the noble it was and his kingly kinsmen
> That afterward conquered kingdoms and came to be lords
> Of well-nigh all the wealth of the Western Isles;
> For royal Romulus to Rome rushed swiftly
> And with great splendor established that first of all cities....

Like all modernizations, the version used here loses all the subtlety. The word *depreced* (line 6) means "subdued" but also faintly suggests "tyrannized"; *bobbaunce* means "boast," glorious or otherwise. Thus in this passage seemingly praising the *athel*, or "noble," Aeneas and his *highe* ("lofty," but perhaps also "high-falutin") kinsmen, the poet subtly undercuts his praise.

The poet's handling of meter has been described in a variety of ways. One theory holds that the standard line follows Old English, having four stresses, thus:

Síþen þe sége and þe assáut watȝ sésed at Troye....

Other theories find eight stresses, seven, four, or five occasionally alternating with four. The last of these theories allows the most natural reading. By this theory the opening of *Sir Gawain* would read roughly as follows:

> Síþen þe sége & þe assáut watȝ sésed at Tróye,
> þe bórȝ bríttened & brént to bróndeȝ & áskeȝ,
> þe túlk þat þe trámmes of trésoun þer wróȝt
> Watȝ tríed for his trícheríe, þe tréwest on érthe.
> Hít watȝ Énnias þe áthel & his híghe kýnde
> þat síþen depréced próuinces, & pátrounes bicóme
> Welnéȝe of ál þe wéle in þe wést íles,
> Fro ríche Rómulus to Róme rícchis hym swýþe;
> With grét bobbáunce þat búrȝe he bíges vpon fýrst,
> & néuenes hit his áune nóme, as hit nów hát....

If we accept this theory, the lines are primarily pentameter, much like blank verse, but are rhythmically more flexible than normal iambic pentameter in that the poet may use more un-stressed syllables than the writer of blank verse could use (cf. Hopkins' "riders"); or he may drop out expected unstressed syllables, because the alliterative poet has a means of signaling his stress pattern when he wishes. By the same means he shifts to a four-stress line. While alliterative signaling is available when the poet wants it, the reader's general expectation of pentameter allows the poet to play games with alliteration when he chooses. Sometimes prefixes may bear the alliteration, even though they are not stressed; sometimes the poet can cross his alliteration, that is, interweave two alliterative patterns in one line:

Me *m*ynez on *o*ne a*m*onge *o*þer, as Ma*þ*ew recordez

or:

*M*yryly on a *f*ayr *m*orn, *m*onyth þe *f*yrst

Or he may use superabundant alliteration:

Whe*þ*er *þ*ay *w*ern *w*orþy *o*þer *w*ers, *w*el *w*ern *þ*ay stowed.

For all his delight in ornamental verse, the poet is a master of realistic dialogue, of controlled tone, and of the sound's seeming echo of the sense.

The poet's style informs not only particular lines but larger dramatic components as well. We have mentioned already his penchant for using symbolic and allegorical devices and his tendency to play with stock "topics" such as the garden which is used in a variety of ways in *Pearl* and later poems in the group. It should be added that, like Chaucer, he is a master of playing one literary genre against another. Professor Benson points out that in the temptation scenes in *Sir Gawain* the poet draws his tempting lady — not only his description of her, but all she says and does, as well as the overall tone of the temptation scenes —

from the medieval genre of *fabliaux,* that is, ribald or earthy stories. The scenes surrounding the temptations, and Gawain's behavior within temptation scenes, come from courtly romance.

The juxtaposition of the two genres results in precisely that controlled confusion necessary at this point in the poem: Gawain cannot tell whether the temptation is serious or mere play—and neither can the reader. In *Pearl* we find a similar crossing of genres. The poem has, on one hand, many of the qualities of a courtly love poem; on the other hand, it is a religious debate.

This same blending of diverse materials may be seen in the poet's manipulation of sources. The clearest example is *Purity,* where we find the unmistakable influence of the *Roman de la Rose; Mandeville's Travels* (in the French version); *Cursor Mundi; The Knight of La Tour-Landry* (probably in French); and the Vulgate Bible. In a complicated plot made up of three linked biblical episodes the poet brings these materials together, associating each episode with the other two by means of puns and verbal repetitions, and at the end of the poem he tells us that he has preached "in three ways" the same moral lesson.

Pearl seems to be constructed in the same way. The story of a man's loss of his child, presumably the actual experience of the poet, is combined with a traditional vision of the unfallen paradise, the Parable of the Vineyard, a discussion of innocence probably drawn from Augustine, and a section of John's *Revelation* to produce a coherent whole.

And in *Sir Gawain* the poet apparently combined two traditional stories, probably the French *Yder* and the *Caradoc,* a story of temptation and a story of beheading, along with a good deal of original material and a few original treatments of stock medieval topics (for instance the turning of the seasons) to form a new whole.

Special mention should be made of the poet's technique in *Pearl,* by far his most complex and perhaps most beautiful poem.

Here the poet uses twelve-line tetrameter stanzas which have both alliteration and a complicated rhyme scheme: *ababababbcbc*. Usually at least three words in a given line alliterate, and the lines are fairly regular, showing the influence of accentual or accentual-syllabic verse. Stanzas are linked by verbal repetition: a key word, either thematically or dramatically significant, appears as the third or fourth stressed word in the final line and again as the first or second stressed word in the first line of the next stanza.

The poet changes the link-word twenty times, dividing the poem into twenty sections, all but one of which contain five linked stanzas. Section XV contains six linked stanzas. It is generally agreed that the poet intended to revise out one of the stanzas in this section (I myself took this point of view in *The Complete Works of the Gawain-poet)*, but there is a strong possibility that the poem is right as it stands. There is not a trace of evidence in *Pearl* that the work was in any sense unfinished, and no looseness in Section XV which would encourage anyone to tamper with the text. The total number of stanzas, 101, is as fitting symbolically as 100 would be, and perhaps more fitting.

The larger order of the poem is as neat as the order of lines and stanzas. The first and last five-stanza sections set up the frame story of the narrator falling asleep in his garden and then, after his dream, awakening. Sections II-IV present physical description of the unfallen paradise, where the narrator finds himself in his dream; Sections V-XIII present the debate between the narrator and the soul of his daughter; and Sections XIV-XIX present visions of the New Jerusalem. In other words, discounting the frame story, *Pearl* treats paradise in three ways, first through images of perfected Nature (trees, hills, birds, etc.); second, through argument and logic; and third, through revelation.

It may be that the poet has in mind the three stages of illumination which Bonaventura has treated in *The Mind's Road to God* – illumination through the senses, through reason, and through mystical leap. Whether or not this is the right explanation, it is clear that *Pearl* is constructed with great care, and no satisfactory account of the poem can ignore the poet's interest in schemata. It may well be that a similar concern for schematic arrangement can be found in other poems of the Pearl group, but if so they have so far eluded critics.

Summaries and Commentaries

PEARL

SECTION I

Stanza 1

In the opening stanza the narrator presents in allegorical fashion the situation which motivates and controls the progress of the poem. His daughter has died, and he cannot stop grieving over his loss. He speaks of the daughter, his emotional treasure, as a pearl worthy of the delight of a prince. He means the phrase, presumably, as an indication of the pearl's extraordinary worth to him, but the phrase ironically suggests the truth which the narrator is not yet able to accept: the child has become the delight of Christ, Prince of all life, whom she has joined in heaven.

This allegorical presentation of matter painful to the narrator is in medieval poetry a standard, and therefore relatively transparent, device. In Chaucer's *Book of the Duchess*, for instance, the Black Knight tells of the death of his lady not in literal terms but through an elaborate artifice which allows him to express deep emotion without unseemly show of grief: he tells Chaucer he lost his queen in a game of chess with Fortune.

The pearl, the narrator says, was one a prince would be pleased to close up purely in a jewel chest of gold, an image which on one level suggests the narrator's love for his child's worth and purity and on another level suggests the literal burial of the child in her casket. The image at the same time looks forward to a later image in the poem, that of heaven as a box of jewels, a place for the safekeeping of souls; but the narrator is not yet ready to understand this implication in his image.

In the first stanza's final quatrain the narrator reveals the source of his grief: the pearl slipped from him, fell into the grass, and vanished. He is pining away, he says, because he is robbed of his love-right (luf-daungere). With the appearance of this phrase the pearl allegory takes on a new dimension: it calls up association with courtly-love poetry, especially that produced in the marguerite-daisy-pearl conventions, in which the marguerite, daisy, or pearl (the emblems are interchangeable) signify the lady. (Cf. Chaucer's Prologue to the *Legend of Good Women*.)

The final line of the first stanza, with its reference to the pearl's lack of any "spot" or flaw insists again on the narrator's sense of his pearl, prepares for the discovery later that the child went immediately to heaven through its purity, and perhaps recalls a line of scripture which might ironically comment on the narrator's attitude — a line which will be echoed repeatedly later in the poem.

Stanza 2

Since the death of his child, the father has often remained near the place where he lost his "pearl," as he continues to call her. Echoing a standard paradox in the poetry of courtly love, he comments that the former cause of all his joy is now the cause of his sorrow; and to this he adds additional paradoxes: he has never heard sweeter music than that which came to him in that still hour as he thought about the child wrapped in clods.

The lines are puzzling, to say the least. E. V. Gordon, in his note on these lines in his edition, explains that "though the poet felt grief, the sweetest of verse would come into his mind. He is evidently describing the genesis of the poem from verses that came to him by the grave, as he pondered his sorrow and the dispensations of God's providence." This explanation is wholly unconvincing, first because God's providence is the farthest thing from the narrator's mind at this point in the poem (he says explicitly in the fifth stanza that he is incapable of listening to reason), and second because it is not verse the poet is talking about but song.

If one looks at the organization of the whole stanza, a different explanation presents itself. The stanza is built on antitheses — static waiting versus active wishing (line 2, original), the child as ender of sorrow versus the child as ender of joy, and, later, "color" versus clods of earth. (In Middle English *color* may suggest not only hue but vitality or spirit as well. The "colors" of rhetoric do not simply prettify; they are said to imbue the subject at hand with life.) The puzzling "song" may be part of another such antithesis:

> þat dotȝ bot þrych my hert þrang,
> My breste in bale bot bolne and bele;
> ȝet þoȝt me neuer so swete a sange
> As stylle stounde let to me stele:
> For soþe þer fleten to me fele.
> To þenke, hir color so clad in clot!

(The punctation of Gordon's edition is changed, though the change is relatively unimportant. A literal translation would read: "That [waiting and wishing] did nothing but afflict my heart, oppressive, and made my breast in sorrow only swell and burn; yet I thought [i.e., imagined or composed] never such a sweet song as that still hour allowed to steal to me: in truth, there floated to me many such! [And] to think, her color was clad [attired] in clods!")

The antithesis, in short, is probably nothing more mysterious than what he experiences on the inside (sorrow and pain) and what he experiences outside — the songs of birds. Bird music is of course a stock element in the medieval garden description (cf. Chaucer's *Book of the Duchess, Parliament of Birds,* or *Legend of Good Women)*; and when the narrator rises in his dream, later in *Pearl,* to the unfallen paradise, where every element of the mutable graveyard garden has its complement in the immutable garden, bird music is one important part of the description.

Stanza 3

The narrator speaks of the flowering spices in the garden and comments that these cannot help but bloom where such richness has gone to corruption. He speaks of yellow, blue, and red blossoms (the standard colors in the conventional garden image) and speaks of how they shine facing the sun. The images set up this far account in two ways for the beauty of the blossoms: they are fed by richness gone to rot, on one hand, and, on the other, they reflect the light of the sun.

The poet now expands this idea: flower and fruit cannot fade where his pearl fell, and this is as it should be; every blade of grass must grow from a dead seed, otherwise no wheat would ever be drawn into barns. Every good has its origin in good; and so, so lovely a seed as the pearl cannot die in the sense that it fails to generate spices — that is, dropping the allegory, new goods in its place. (This reading takes "fede" in the original, "Flor and fryte may not be fede," to mean faded, not, as some scholars would read it, "fed." The reading "fed," though it has been elaborately defended, makes only farfetched sense.)

This stanza — one of the most beautiful in the poem — further develops the antithesis, set up in the preceding stanza, between the poet's emotion and the world outside him: though he grieves, birds sing and flowers bloom. He makes of Nature's beauty a desperate rationalization: the good must decay if new goods are to come. She is not dead after all, she lives on in Nature. But the answer is, as always, inadequate. Set by itself, the line "So semly a sede moȝt fayly not" expresses the narrator's true emotion — "So lovely a seed cannot fail" — but the continuation of the thought in the next line sadly undercuts it — cannot fail in that spices do not rise out of it.

The child's living on in Nature is not enough to satisfy human love; there must be a better answer. Like a secret, the stanza contains that answer. The image of the sun, emblem of God though in itself "dim and blue" by comparison to God's light (as the poet says later) points the direction. The wheat brought to the barn, if read as traditional Christian allegory, suggests God's wheat, the souls of the good, drawn to the store-house of heaven. God is the true good in whom all lesser goods have their genesis, and heaven is the true pearl, though the narrator is not yet ready to understand. The child's death, read allegorically, is part of God's harvest, the subject of the first quatrain of the next stanza and also one of the subjects of the Parable of the Vineyard which will enter the poem later.

Stanza 4

"Once," the narrator says, "I entered that treed garden ["erber"] in August, in the ripe season when grain is cut with keen sickles. If the place was beautiful with all its blooming spices [medieval peonies are also spices, not, as now, flamboyant little flowers], the scent was even more beautiful." The shadow-covered grave with blossoming plants above and around it, the whole plot bathed in incense, is a worthy dwelling place for the pearl, the narrator says. The narrator is right, insofar as the graveyard plot allegorically suggests the true dwelling place of the pearl, the spice-filled, unfallen paradise he will explore in his dream; but the beauty of the literal graveyard is no comfort for grief.

Stanza 5

The narrator wrings his hands, caught up in icy sorrow, and the misery dinning in his heart blocks his reason. Though he knows that the nature and example of Christ ought to comfort him—a nature higher than the Nature around him—his will labors in woe. He sinks to the ground, the scent of the spices overcomes him, and he loses consciousness. The final image in this stanza is curious. The spices are obviously literal plants in a literal garden. But spices are also, traditionally, an image of grace, and certainly the narrator's dream is a true celestial vision. And so it seems that here lower and higher nature work together, in other words, that physical reality is shot through with spiritual reality. The idea is a commonplace of medieval thought, but the narrator's swoon is nevertheless a striking treatment of the idea.

SECTION II

The narrator finds himself walking in spirit, his body left in the graveyard behind him, in a marvelous place where there are crystal cliffs, huge jewels in place of rocks, holtwoods with boles of indigo, beautiful flowers, and so forth. This passage and others like it in this poem express superbly the joy medieval men took in splendid artifice emblematic of what Yeats called the "artifice of eternity." The stanza-line word "adubbemente" is central to the feeling of the section. It means "adornment," "resplendency," and so forth, but it has the overtone or nuance of beauty brought about through the transmutation of something lower. At least in theory, a man who is "dubbed" knight is not merely adorned with a title: his very character is changed or at least fixed at its noblest level.

It is not surprising, then, that the imagery of this section is art imagery: the leaves on the trees slide like polished silver and "trill" (both musically and visually?) on the branches when the light of the sun, breaking through the patches of blue between clouds, glides over them; the birds in this forest sing more beautifully than any human instrumentalist can play; no poet on earth would be equal to the task of describing the beauty of the place; the banks of the river are like gold thread (in a tapestry). The very landscape, like a medieval baron's estate, is ordered by art: hedges, borders, rivers. And the jewels in the riverbed are like glints through glass. In all this artifice, one contrasting image stands out, the climactic image of the section: the jewels in the riverbed are also like "streaming stars when earthlings sleep, which stare [shine] in the welkin on a winter night."

SECTION III

The narrator walks on, drawn by the joy of seeing "more and more," the refrain link in this section. He gradually realizes that he is in Paradise, and he begins to hunt eagerly for a ford which will allow him to cross the jeweled stream; but the farther he goes, the higher the banks become. At last he discovers a maiden at the foot of a bank across the stream and recognizes her.

The focus of this section is chiefly on the emotion of the narrator—his sense of joy, at first, which accords with the beauty of the landscape; then his frustration as he tries to find a crossing place; finally his mingled shock, fear, and longing when it becomes clear to him (little by little, as can happen in dreams) that the maiden across from him is his daughter.

SECTION IV

Tempted to call out to his child, the father holds back for fear of frightening her away and simply looks at her mysterious attire. She is dressed in clothes sewn all over with pearls, has a crown of pearls on which flowers are fashioned out of joined pearls, and has one huge and flawless pearl on her breast. She bows, offering to speak with the narrator, and he is overjoyed. The imagery is striking, throughout this section. In the opening stanza both the narrator's fear of calling out and his fear that the child may escape him are presented in hawking images: "With eyes open and mouth completely closed, I stood as quiet as a hawk in the hall," the narrator says; and "I feared what might happen if she should escape me, the one I saw there, before I might by a call bring her to stop [or meet with her]." The description of the pearl-studded garb which follows is incredibly rich — in sound, in emotional response to artificial elegance (such dress actually existed in the Middle Ages), and in brilliant imagery (for instance the girl's hair, line 213, which is like newly cut gold). At last the child acknowledges the dreamer's presence, making it possible for him to speak.

SECTION V

The narrator movingly tells the child of his grief since she vanished. He has mourned for her alone at night, he says, since she slipped into the grass. Ironically, she has landed ("lyʒte") on the earth of Paradise, where she is completely happy while he is, as he says, a "joyless jeweler." Surprisingly, the child answers him scornfully, twisting his image. This garden is a perfect jewel box: if he were a proper jeweler he would be grateful to have his pearl so safely locked up. She shifts to legal language, arguing that if he would lose *all* his joy for one gem, he has come to plead a foolish cause. What he has lost was only a rose, a natural flower which bloomed and died as nature demanded; but by the nature or *kind* (a sort of pun in Middle English, suggesting both "nature" and "natural kindness") of the box enclosing the dead rose it is changed to a precious pearl. The jeweler has called his fate a thief (the idea of a court plea is maintained by the image), though fate has made "ought of nought"; he accuses the remedy of his mishap and must therefore be no natural or kind jeweler.

The dreamer sees that the child is right—her words are jewels—and tries to apologize. He asks to be excused and promises that from now on all will be well: having found his pearl he will remain with her and will love his Lord and all His laws that have brought him so close to his bliss. He would be a joyful jeweler, he says, if only he were with his pearl beyond the waterway. But again the pearl rebuffs him, this time calling him insane. He has made three mistakes: he says he knows her to be near merely because with his untrustworthy mortal eyes he sees her, as he supposes; he says he will dwell with her; and he suggests that he will cross the waterway, a thing no "joyful" mortal jeweler can do.

SECTION VI

The pearl mocks the jeweler's willingness to trust his naked eye, again ironically twisting his image. She perhaps means both that a true jeweler in this world knows better than to judge gems without a glass for close inspection and that the mortal eye is never sufficient in spiritual matters. He is "uncourteous," that is, churlish and disrespectful, ignorant of the ways of *court,* to believe his Lord would lie. God has promised to raise man though Fortune (here the natural world under God) kills him. A man who correctly places God above the realm of Fortune would know better than to trust nothing but what he sees. To put faith in his own skill above faith in God is an act of pride. Commenting on his second and third mistakes, his assertion that he will stay with her in her place across the river, the pearl points out that he ought to ask permission at least— and even then he would fail. Before he can enter, his body must die, for it was forfeited in Eden.

The dreamer cries out against this just abuse: the child is dooming him to sorrow again, forcing him to lose what he has just found. What good is treasure—in this case a treasured love— if it serves merely to make men grieve when it is lost? The pearl answers that he thinks of nothing but sorrow and asks him why. Very often from grief at some small loss, she says, men throw away more. Better to bless oneself and love God, for anger gains nothing. She illustrates this with a striking hunting image. Ulti- mately man must be like the trapped doe who thrashes and brays but at last learns that she cannot escape and so becomes patient and silent, waiting to see what the hunter will choose to do, free her or kill her (in some seasons the doe was spared by medieval hunters, in other seasons not). God will not budge a foot from his purpose, at least while man tries to force Him to move; one can only ask mercy.

SECTION VII

The dreamer at last becomes reasonable. He confesses that he has been raving because of the grief which rolls from him like water from a well and asks that if he speaks foolishly she will have mercy on him, remembering that formerly she stood be- tween him and grief. While she was removed from every peril, he was full of misery, having no idea where his pearl had gone. They were as one when they parted; it would be a pity if they were to be cross with each other now that they "meet so seldom by stick [tree] or stone." The dreamer adds that he is only a mortal and may naturally fail in the "manners" appropriate to heaven's court—an idea the poet will develop in detail, showing the disparity between ideal "courtesy" and the "courtesy" of earth. His only hope, he says, lies in Christ's mercy "and Mary and John"—an image suggesting the common medieval emblem of Christ, Mary, and John at the crucifixion, a figure of human sorrow softened by God's love.

Now the dreamer asks that, without further disagreement or "debate," he be allowed to ask about the pearl's manner of life. Pleased with his altered manner, the pearl agrees. Pride and masterful spirit are not approved here, she tells him: when he comes before his Lord he should show meek devotion. She then presents a seeming paradox. Though she was a child of tender age when she died, she is now bride to Christ himself and crowned a queen to live out all the days of eternity, joined to his heritage.

SECTION VIII

The dreamer is astonished and distressed, understanding the child's rise in fortune in earthly rather than heavenly terms. He has understood that the Virgin is queen of heaven, a woman so unique in virtue that she is called the Phoenix of Araby. The child kneels, at the dreamer's mention of the Virgin's name, and praises her, then rises and explains. There are no usurpers in heaven, and the Virgin is indeed empress of all heaven, earth, and hell, and known as the Queen of Courtesy. But everyone who arrives in the court of God is king or queen of all the realm yet deprives no other of the same honor; and the Virgin is queen above all others. Then (following Paul) she compares the order of heaven to the order of the human body, wherein all members work together, the head, for instance, feeling no spite toward the finger which wears a fine ring.

The dreamer, still confused by his knowledge of the way of mere earthly courts, continues to misunderstand; he complains that the system is unfair, since a young child ought not to win the same honor as those who suffered for God through a long life.

SECTIONS IX-X

The child knew neither her "Our Father" nor her Creed at the time of her death, yet she has been made a queen on the first day. The dreamer cannot understand how she might rise so quickly, though he might understand her being made, say, a countess. The child answers by retelling the Parable of the Vineyard, making it (in traditional medieval fashion) a lesson on grace and works, or, in the poem's terms, purity and patience. The interest in the retelling of the familiar story is chiefly in the lyricism of the verse and what might be called the realism of detail. The work of the harvest, the dialogue of the owner, the "reeve" and the workers, and the like are all presented in life-like fashion. But the poet's use of the parable is interesting in another way as well: the harvest image picks up the earlier image of the August garden which opened the poem, and throws new light on that image. What appeared a death was in fact God's harvest.

The moral the pearl draws from the parable reinforces her earlier remark that man can get nothing from God by demanding his "rights." She has gotten more than anyone could get by asking for what he deserves. Again the dreamer objects, insisting that unless all scripture is a lie, God gives men what they earn.

SECTION XI

The pearl's answer is that no distinction can be made between "more" and "less" when the gift is infinite. Picking up the dreamer's image of his sorrow which flowed like water from a well, she describes God's gifts as like water flooding from a drain or ditch. The water of Grace (the counterpart and resolution of the wellings of sorrow) is immeasurable. Moreover, the pearl adds, where was there ever a person who, living out a long life, did not sometime act or think amiss? The sinner can only ask mercy—God's grace. The innocent, on the other hand, have been washed in the water of baptism (a figure for Grace) then directly lifted to heaven. She reminds the dreamer that man lost his right to perfect paradise when he bit an apple in Eden, but later there came an antidote, the blood of Christ. Out of the "well" of Christ's wounds came the water of baptism and the blood of redemption, which lift man out of the death in which he formerly had to "drown." (The well image will be used in still other ways later in the poem.)

SECTIONS XII-XIII

The pearl continues her explanation, pointing out that Jesus has said that no one can enter heaven unless he comes as a child, unspotted by sin: this (heaven) is the pearl of price for which the "jeweler" of the parable sold all his earthly goods, a pearl which is owned in common by all who are righteous. She adds (mysteriously) that it is set here on her breast. Then, interpreting the image of earthly goods – the "wool and linen" of the parable – she advises the dreamer to forsake the mad world and buy the spotless pearl.

The dreamer now asks who formed the child's flawless figure and in asking it develops a stock rhetorical figure of the Middle Ages (she was never formed by Pygmalion, never reckoned by Aristotle, etc. – cf. the opening of Chaucer's *Physician's Tale* for another treatment of the rhetorical devices). She answers that she was formed by the flawless Lamb, Christ. Seeing no flaw in her, he called her to himself, washed her apparel in his blood, crowned her, and set the pearl on her breast, making her his wife. Again the dreamer cannot understand and asks why she rather than another should be made Christ's wife: how could she drive out all the others who were precious to Christ, boldly making herself his matchless and flawless queen?

SECTIONS XIV-XV

She corrects him. She is flawless, but not matchless. The brides of Christ number 144,000, as John reported in Revelations. She reminds him of John's vision of Christ's brides on Zion, the New City of Jerusalem, and contrasts the Old Jerusalem, where Christ was slain. She tells the story, quoting from both John and Isaiah, of how Christ went silently to his death for the love of man. Like the wine-lord of the parable, Christ comes each day for his own (line 847), and all are perfectly – therefore equally – happy. Paraphrasing John, she tells how Christ and his brides, the risen Church, celebrate around the throne and how music falls on all sides like a flood (line 874).

In this passage various earlier images are echoed and later images prepared. The angelic harpers and singers recall the earlier birds of paradise and the music in the graveyard-garden; the flood of music recalls the earlier flood images and prepares for the vision later of Grace rumbling through the streets of the New Jerusalem; the dreamer's image of his child as a rose (in line 906) recalls the earlier image of the natural rose transformed to a "figured rose" made of pearls and prepares for the image of the risen church as a "garland"; and so on. In the final stanza of Section XV, the dreamer begs permission to ask one thing more.

SECTION XVI

The narrator asks to see the pearl's dwelling place. He understands about Jerusalem, where David had his throne, he says; but here by these woods he sees no buildings or castle walls. Surely there must be some great city nearby to contain so many; it would be unnatural that pearls should be left to lie outdoors. The pearl explains again that there are two Jerusalems and with ingenious puns on Middle English "mote" — which can mean walled city (cf. modern "moat"), can mean spot or stain, and can mean dispute — re-emphasizes the difference.

SECTIONS XVII-XVIII

She tells the dreamer to walk beside her, across the stream, up the hill before him. He starts out in haste and sees just what John saw in his revelation: the heavenly city built all of gems; streets of gold as clean as glass; walls twelve furlongs wide, long, and high; three doors on each wall, each bearing the name of one of the twelve tribes of Israel. The city is brighter than either the sun or moon and has no need of such lesser lights, being lit by the light of God Himself. At the center of the city the dreamer sees God on His throne, a river running from the throne's base, brighter than any earthly light. He sees no church in the city, for God Himself is the church there, and Christ himself is the refreshment. Along the river of Grace he sees glowing

trees which bear "the twelve fruits of life" twelve months a
year, eternally renewed. (cf. Bonaventura's *The Tree of Life.*)
Before this splendor, the dreamer stands like "a dazed quail,"
knowing that no earthly body could bear the power of that vision.

SECTION XIX

While he is looking at the city he is suddenly aware—just
as one may be suddenly aware of the risen moon before the fall
of darkness—of a wonderful procession of all Christ's virgins,
each one dressed as was his child. He then sees the Lamb himself with his seven golden horns and his apparel as white as
pearl, sees the aldermen bow before him, sees legions of angels
scatter incense, and hears their song to the "beautiful jewel"
Christ. The dreamer further describes Christ and cries out in
anguish at the sight of his terrible wound. Nevertheless, Christ
and all his company are supremely joyful. At last the dreamer
sees his own child, and he is so overcome by joy and "love-
longing" at the sight that he resolves to cross the stream and
join her.

SECTION XX

With joy driving in through his eyes and ears, the dreamer is
maddened and in this state imagines that nothing can stop him
from crossing to heaven: despite any blow, he will swim across
or die—and will win his desire either way. He stirs to leap into
the stream and, in stirring, wakes himself. And so at last he re-
signs himself to God's will. If it is true that the pearl is now in
that "beautiful garland," heaven, then he will be satisfied with
his mournful dungeon, earth. All his life, he recalls, he has tried
to serve God loyally, but he foolishly wanted more than man can
have, and so he has been corrected. He resolves to strive now to
be a loyal Christian and prays that he and all men may be God's
humble household servants, precious pearls which are pleasing
to God. Thus he at last accepts, however mournfully, the lesson
of Christ's parable of the vineyard, recognizing that what his

pearl won by purity he must win by patient devotion. From unearthly vision he has fallen to humble acceptance of earthly emblems of that vision, Christ who is symbolically revealed by the priest in the form of bread and wine.

In admitting his station as humble servant to God he has come to understand true "courtesy," that is, man's role in the lowest station of the metaphysical court of God. Because God's lordship is absolute, man must renounce the three errors pointed out by the pearl and dramatically represented throughout the poem — the intellectual pride which makes man believe he knows better than God, the pride of spirit which makes man imagine he can force God to kindness, and the pride of boundless desire. It was madness (confused intellect) which made the dreamer think he could outwit God and cross the stream; it was misguided courage which caused him to make the attempt; and it was wrongful desire that motivated his action. Christian patience, then, comes with "right reason" — acceptance of God's judgment, steadfast loyalty instead of misguided courage or force, and reasonable rather than unreasonable desire.

PURITY

The second poem in the Pearl group, *Purity*, elaborates the idea of purity sketched out in *Pearl* and further develops, as a secondary theme, the idea of patience. It is a poem constructed of interwoven biblical stories with transitional materials from other sources. The general focus of the poem is on God's punishments of the impure, on one hand, the impatient, on the other; in other words it emphasizes God's dangerous justice. (The following poem in the group, *Patience*, presents the other side of the coin, God's mercy toward sinners.) The difference between God's punishment of the impatient and his punishment of the impure is that in the first case his punishment is carefully measured: it amounts to a withdrawal of his gifts. In the second case he punishes with wrath.

The poem opens with a direct statement of God's wrath toward those who, serving him, are found unclean. The poet takes priests as an example, arguing that they have enormous power if they serve God loyally but are loathed if they do not. In His heavenly court God is served by spotless angels; it is therefore natural that he should detest fouler servants. He will endure near Himself no soul "gone dark with sin"—an image which prepares for the later image of a pearl gone dark and in need of renewal in wine. To show the justice of God's wrath toward the impure, the poet compares God's response to the unclean to the response of an ordinary earthly ruler to foulness in his court. If some churl were to come in rags and tatters before a ruler dressed in his finest and seated among his dukes on the dais eating dinner, the ruler would certainly be outraged and would have the man thrown out, telling him never to return on pain of imprisonment or worse.

The poet then tells the story of the lord who prepared a wedding feast for his son and invited in all his old friends (a parable from Matthew). The emphasis in the poet's brilliantly realistic retelling of the story is first of all on the naturalness of the lord's wrath, second on the allegorical meaning. On the level of allegory, the story tells what will happen to Jews (false vassals who renounce their lord, in the medieval view), to true Christians, and to false Christians. The poet reinforces the allegory by introducing new imagery such as the underground dungeon "where sorrow dwells forever."

On the literal level, the focus of the story is not on the justice but on the naturalness of the lord's wrath. The lord's behavior is seen from the outset as exceptional, for the poet has already presented the norm—the ragged churl who would be thrown out with a warning. The difference between normal behavior and the behavior of the baron in the parable is that the baron is unusually angry. He has been insulted by his friends and now he is insulted by a stranger, a man who (as it seems to the baron, at any rate) has made no pretense of cleaning himself up or dressing for the feast.

If it is to be expected that an earthly lord will be furious when his efforts to spread a pleasing feast are mocked and marred by discourtesy in the normal sense (bad manners), how much more it is to be expected that God will be stirred to wrath by discourtesy in the extended sense, which is superficially similar but more dreadful in its effects, man's willful and scornful perversion of the order of the universe. The poet now spells out what he means by this greater impurity or sullying of the soul: sloth, pride, covetousness, treachery, perjury, murder, gluttony, and so forth.

He then distinguishes between degrees of sin. Sins of impatience, that is, sins based on the vassal's unwillingness to behave as a vassal, lead to tempered punishment, while sins of impurity lead to worse. He tells the stories of Lucifer's fall and Adam's—both falls of impatience—and contrasts the measured punishments in these cases with God's wrathful punishment of Noah's generation, who through sexual perversion created monsters. The poet tells this third story at considerable length and with great power, a story filled with vividly imagined particulars and superb rhetoric. At the end of the story he briefly moralizes it, returning to his original theme, that no man can come before God who is not spotless, "Without macule or mote, like a Marjory pearl."

Then, after a brief transition, he tells a second story of God's wrathful destruction, this time the destruction of Sodom and Gomorrah. Again he tells the story at length, with a wealth of realistic detail. He closes the story with a superb description, both literal and allegorical, of the dead sea, a figure of hell. (The source is Mandeville's *Travels.*) Then comes another transition. He borrows the argument from the *Roman de la Rose* that to win a lady's love one must imitate her virtue, and argues that this must be even truer in the case of the man who would win God's love.

He comments on the spiritual (and physical) cleanness of Christ's nativity, tells how his cleanness drove out the foulness of lepers and the like, and refers in passing to the legend, familiar in the Middle Ages, that Christ's fingers were so "clean" (this time in the sense of *precise*) that he could break bread more perfectly with his hands than with a knife. The poet then spells out the way in which sinful man may become clean again — renewed like a pearl. As a pearl is renewed by wine when it has become sullied by use in the world, the soul can be polished by faithful confession. Once confessed, the poet says, man must be careful to remain faithful to God, for once a vessel has been made sacred to God, He is outraged if it is thrown to the ground.

The double sense of "vessel" — on the literal level a cup or dish, on the allegorical level a man given to God, a "vessel of the holy spirit" — prepares the way for the third story of God's wrathful destruction, His overthrow of Belshazzar. When Israel lapsed in faith, God allowed Nebuchadnezzar to conquer the people and sack the temple, taking away the treasured vessels. Nebuchadnezzar came to be converted to Jehovah, but his son Belshazzar returned to the worship of graven images. He was thus both a sullied vessel himself and (as one who reveled with the holy vessels of the temple) a man who befouled vessels. The poet retells the whole story with the same power and realism he has achieved in his stories of Noah and Sodom. In his closing lines the poet says that he has now shown in three ways how impurity is overthrown by the wrath of God, while purity leads to eternal bliss.

The chief interest of *Purity* is the poet's powerful retelling of the Bible stories, but it has other kinds of interest as well. The three central stories are interrelated as we have said, by verbal repetition and imagistic echo, and all three are given allegorical extension. Lucifer and his legions fall, like the rain in Noah's time, for forty days, and the significance of the wicked angels' fall is extended by a startling image in which they are compared to the dust of sifted grain — they are, in effect, chaff, separated from the grain, emblematic of God's chosen. The contrast between the courteous Noah and the discourteous remainder of mankind is reflected in a contrast between Noah's white, loyal dove and his black, rebellious raven, one identified with the Holy Ghost, the other with Lucifer.

The initial story of the wedding feast, symbolic of the feast of the blessed in the New Jerusalem, is re-echoed in the poet's emphasis on feasts as he tells the story of Sodom. He tells first of the feast Abraham prepares for the Lord, then of Lot's feast for the two visiting angels; and he develops a striking contrast between the behavior of Abraham's wife Sarah and the behavior of Lot's wife. Sarah is slightly "impatient" in the medieval sense — in other words, she is less than nimble in obedience and at one point laughs at God; but she does obey, however grudgingly, and she is pure. Lot's wife disobeys Lot and introduces an impurity — salt — into the food for the angels. Later, with impure desire, she looks back to Sodom and is punished.

There is also a contrast between the barrenness of Sarah, which God will turn into an antitype of Noah's flood (the heirs who "fall" from Abraham shall "flood" the world) and the situation of Lot's wife, who bears two daughters and then becomes, like the hills around Sodom, sterile stone and salt forever. Inferno imagery is to be found everywhere in the destruction scene; and, in contrast, Lot's flight with his two "lily-white" daughters is to a "hill" where, as Abraham learns later, *"he is on lofte wonnen"* — he dwells aloft.

In the third story, Belshazzar's feast is an antitype of the heavenly feast allegorically described in the parable which opens the poem: the jewels mentioned in connection with Belshazzar's feast — the jewels on the holy vessels — recall the apocalyptic vision of heaven in *Pearl:* Belshazzar's castle surrounded by water recalls Noah's ark, an emblem of heaven or the risen Church; like the heavenly castle in *Pearl,* Belshazzar's castle is "square," but whereas the true castle is built of twelves, Belshazzar's is built of sevens (a number of Nature or man-in-Nature.)

As the poem progresses the focus narrows from all mankind to a particular kingdom to a particular man. Another kind of progression is also apparent. Noah's generation engenders monsters, deforming Nature in general; the homosexual Sodomites defile themselves and other men, and defile Nature only incidentally; and Belshazzar defiles, above all, himself.

PATIENCE

In the third poem in the group, *Patience,* the dominant theme is patience; the theme of purity is now subdominant. On the literal level the poem tells of the impatience of Jonah, which contrasts with the lordly patience of God, who tolerates mistakes in his vassal. On the level of allegory Jonah's impatience contrasts with the perfect patience of Christ (a common medieval idea) and, at the same time, parallels the impatience of Satan.

Told to go to Nineveh, Jonah fears that the Ninevites might strip him to the skin and hang him on a cross in the company of thieves; the belly of the whale, where Jonah stays for three days and nights (the amount of time Christ spent in hell), is explicitly compared to Sheol, and the stink there is explicitly the stench of hell.

But if he is disloyal, he is not impure: in the belly of the whale he remains as pure as possible, the poet says. He is of course unable to remain completely pure in such a place, and when the whale vomits Jonah up, the poet comments: "Well it might be that the robe he wore needed washing," a quibble on being washed in Christ's blood upon entering heaven—as the child was washed in *Pearl.* Like *Purity,* the poet's retelling of the Jonah story is remarkable for its vivid realism. It is remarkable, too, for its characterization of the grumbling, miserable Jonah.

SIR GAWAIN AND THE GREEN KNIGHT

Sir Gawain and the Green Knight can easily be read as a further exploration of the interrelated themes, purity and patience, which have informed the Pearl group thus far. Sir Gawain is a Virgin-serving knight, famous for "love talking" but apparently unacquainted with the kind of love the lady at

Hautdesert Castle attempts to force on him; and as a knight he is the very emblem of faithful vassalage implied by the concept of patience. But the poem is too complex—and too controversial in its meaning—to be adequately treated in terms of purity and patience alone. It may therefore be best to deal with it, as we dealt with *Pearl*, by close paraphrase and running commentary.

PART ONE

Stanza 1

The poem begins, as it will end, with an allusion to the fall of Troy and the flight of the Trojan heroes into Europe, where each founded a new kingdom. The opening stanza brilliantly sets up the cycle of death and rebirth which will control the whole action of the poem: after telling of the total destruction of Troy, the poet tells of splendid beginnings of new civilizations—in Rome, in Tuscany, in Lombardy, and finally in Britain. But the pivotal short line, *"wyth wynne"*—with joy—prepares for an irony. The nation established "with joy" is one where "war and wrack and wonder" have come since.

Stanza 2

Bold warriors have been bred up in Britain from the first, and more marvels have been met there than anywhere else. The greatest of the British kings was Arthur, and the poet declares his intention of telling one of the strangest of the Arthur stories, and to tell it in the ancient traditional fashion (in alliterative verse), just as he "heard it told in town." It is highly unlikely that the poet actually heard the story, instead of making it up on the basis of hints in older stories. Medieval poets characteristically claim their stories are borrowed from some authority; probably no one in the audience took the claim seriously.

Stanza 3

The poet tells of Arthur's Christmas festivities at Camelot— jousts, dances, feasts—an assemblage of the greatest lords and ladies who ever lived. The king was the handsomest that ever reigned, for all the people there were in their first (presumably untested) youth.

Stanza 4

Now the poet narrows his scene to the New Year's feast: the people have just come from mass for gift-giving games of some obscure nature, possibly some form of handy-dandy comparable to the gift game which occurs later at Hautdesert Castle, in the forest. After the gift-giving the company all goes to dinner, where they sit, with Guinevere in the center, on a blazing dais which has a tapestry-tent spangled with gems. The fairest of all the gems, the poet says, is the queen herself. Standing alone, the description here is simply of a marvelous feast; but in the context of the whole Pearl group it has a slightly ironic ring. Details here and later echo details in the earlier description of Belshazzar's feast, and the emphasis on gems—and on Guinevere as a gem—may ironically recall to mind the similar emphasis on gems and a lady as gem in *Pearl*. The poet may intend, in other words, a hint that the feast has about it a slightly dangerous worldiness, Camelot being a sort of earthly paradise, possibly a false paradise, or, at all events, that Arthur's court, in its innocent delight in things worldly, is overconfident.

Stanza 5

Arthur is characterized as slightly boyish, a man too restless to sit or lie down for long at a time; but the poet adds in haste that Arthur has also another reason for waiting until all the others are served: he has made a vow that he will not begin eating at the New Year's festival until he has heard some strange news or until someone has come to challenge the court. He stands "bold in his place," a phrase slightly ironic in the original (*stif in stalle*, a comic variation on the common alliterative phrase *stif in stede*, loosely, "bold on the battlefield," as Miss Borroff has observed). The point of the gentle humor seems to be, again, the untested nature of the court.

Stanzas 6-7

The poet mentions the seating arrangement at the main table, as he will again describe the seating arrangement at Hautdesert Castle; then he tells in glowing terms of the marvelous foods and the music which introduces them. Then a rather different music comes which enables Arthur himself to eat: an enormous man comes galloping into the hall. He is handsomely formed, almost a giant; and he is entirely green.

Stanzas 8-10

The poet describes the green man's dress – a cloak and hood of fine furs, tightly stretched hose, leather riding-guards, gems on his belt and saddle, all of green. The horse he rides is also green interwoven with gold. The man has a huge beard and hair clipped as an elf's would be. His eyes flash like lightning, and the court surmises that any man who dared to go against him would have little chance of winning. Yet he is not dressed in armor and has no shield. Instead, he carries a holly branch, a symbol that he comes in peace, and in the other hand carries a great ax, which the poet describes in detail. The man comes galloping straight to the king's table, hailing no one, and there asks which of the nobles is Arthur. He studies them all, mockingly pretending he cannot tell which of them is the king.

Stanzas 11-12

No one answers. Instead, each man wonders what on earth this may mean, stares at the mysterious green, and sits astounded at the huge man's voice. They suppose it must all be some magic or illusion, and all sounds in the court die as if the nobles had suddenly fallen asleep, a hint that they may indeed have been put into a spell by magic. But some – the poet hastily adds – probably kept still not from fright but from courtesy, since this was Arthur's hall, not theirs.

At last Arthur answers, welcoming the stranger and inviting him to join the feast and to ask later whatever it is he has come to ask. The green man refuses the invitation and tells the Round Table that he has come because he has heard of the court's great reputation. He could have come dressed to fight if he had wanted, he says, but he comes only for a little game. Arthur, supposing he means a duel, assures him that he will get what he asks. The whole of the green man's speech on the glory of the Round Table has an obviously hollow ring. As one critic points out, he sounds throughout like an adult lightly mocking children. In fact, the Green Knight will call them children in a moment.

Stanza 13

The green man denies that he is after a duel, since here on this bench he can see only beardless children. What he does ask is an exchange of strokes with the ax, and he will allow his adversary the first stroke. He cheerfully urges them to take up the challenge, promising to give the ax to the man who does so, and he stipulates that between the first stroke and the second a twelvemonth and a day shall pass. The stipulated time span is of course another detail supporting the idea, first suggested in the opening stanza, of cyclical corruption and regeneration—an idea which will later take the form of a fall and a renewal through confession and penance.

Stanzas 14-15

Again the court is silent. The green man stirs impatiently and rolls his red eyes, then ahems as if in embarrassment. He mocks the cowardice of this court so famous for derring-do, then laughs outright. Arthur is furious, blushes, and draws near. Though he claims to find the challenge ridiculous, he accepts it himself, leaps to the green man, seizes the gisarme, and swings it over his head as if to strike. Calmly, the green man bares his neck and waits. Then Gawain asks that the game be given to him.

Stanza 16

In what sounds like an outrageous parody of polite courtly speech, Gawain asks permission to leave Guinevere's side, provided she doesn't mind, and asks the advice and consent of his fellow knights, claiming that he is the least of them in value and granting that perhaps his request is silly. They must be the judge. The knights accept his request and advise that the king turn the game over to Gawain.

The poet's introduction of his hero sets the tone for the whole of Gawain's story. The young man is unquestionably generous and noble, but he is just as unquestionably amusing in his mingled innocence and sophistication.

Stanzas 17-18

Gawain takes the weapon from Arthur; the king blesses him and urges Gawain to strike heartily, for if he does the return stroke will not trouble him much. The green man asks Gawain to rehearse the terms of the agreement and asks him his name. Gawain tells him his name and repeats the terms. The Green Knight is delighted. When Gawain asks where the Green Knight can be found when the time comes, the Green Knight stalls him, saying that it will be soon enough to tell him after the ax stroke, provided he survives it.

Stanzas 19-20

Then the Green Knight gets into position. Gawain braces himself, then strikes with all his might. The head falls from the body and rolls under the feet of the people at the feast, who kick it away in horror. But the green man does not fall. He runs after the head, seizes it and holds it up, then leaps onto his horse. He holds the head by the hair and it speaks. The head tells Gawain to seek until he finds the Green Chapel but does not tell where the chapel can be found. He gives a final warning that if Gawain fails he will be known everywhere as a coward; then he gallops away. Gawain and the king stare at each other and, though they are astounded, laugh.

Stanza 21

Arthur is distressed, but he lets no sign of his distress show. To Guinevere, he dismisses the event as an "interlude" — a courtly masque of a sort—but adds that now he may indeed begin his meal, for certainly he's seen a marvel. Gawain hangs up the ax where all men may see it, and the king and his knight turn to the feast. Day passes and darkness comes. The poem's first part ends with a dark warning by the poet: "Beware, Gawain, that you not end a betrayer of your bargain through fear." Thus this section of the poem, which began in half-ironic, lighthearted talk about the honor of a court whose value has not yet been proved, concludes with a deadly earnest warning against lapsing from honor—or, in the terms of the Pearl group as a whole, a warning against a knight's lapsing from "patience," in this case a knight's loyalty to the ideal he serves.

PART TWO

Stanzas 1-2

The opening stanzas of Part Two put the whole of Part One in a new light. What originally seemed noble in the king now seems foolish: Gawain's sad plight is the result of the king's foolish yearning to hear men boast; what originally seemed a merry game now seems a grim mistake which the knights made because they'd had too much to drink. A year turns quickly, the poet says, and the ending is seldom like the beginning. He then describes, with splendid imagistic detail, the turning of the seasons. After winter, rain comes and flowers bloom and trees blossom; then summer comes, the plants rejoice; but soon the harvest season comes, warning plants to ripen quickly, for winter is on its way; then cold winds tear the leaves from the trees and the grass that was once bright green turns drab, and at last all that once flourished comes to rot. The focal point in the whole description is on trees and grass and the effect of weather upon them. The ominous overtone is clear: flesh is grass. What has happened in a year to the plants may happen to Gawain as well. He recalls his gloomy mission.

Stanzas 3-7

Gawain spends the Christmastime feast with Arthur and the Round Table, and all the lords and ladies pretend to be merry for Gawain's sake, though they are secretly grieved that they must lose him forever, as they think. After the meal Gawain asks permission to leave the king and his lords. He calls for his armor, and the poet describes the process of his arming. When the arming is complete, Gawain attends mass, then goes for his final leave-taking. His horse Gringolet is now ready, also splendidly armed. Gawain takes his magnificently adorned helmet, crowned with diamonds.

Finally he is given his shield, which the poet describes at length. On the outside it has a five-pointed star, the "Pentangle," or "endless knot," a symbol perfectly appropriate for Gawain. Each point represents five virtues: he is faultless in his five senses, unfailing in his five fingers, devoted to Christ's five wounds (received on the Cross), and supported by the five joys of Mary, and he is a master of five virtues – generosity, good fellowship, purity, courtesy, and charity. (The pentangle is also, traditionally, a symbol used to ward off black magic.) On the inside of the shield he has an image of the Virgin, who gives him strength in battle.

As Professor Don Howard has pointed out (see Selected Bibliography), the shield is one of the two chief symbols in the poem, summing up Gawain's inner and outer knightly character. The outside of the shield – the side others see – shows the virtues and talents with which he defends social and religious order; the inside – the side Gawain sees – is a reminder of that humility and otherworldliness which ought to preserve him from involvement in the worldly order he defends. In the light of the Pearl group as a whole, the outside might be seen as an emblem of Gawain's *patience* – his loyal service of those above and below him in the social order – while the inside is emblematic of that *purity* of heart which gives him strength.

At last Gawain seizes his lance and sets off on his quest for the Green Chapel, believing he will never return.

Stanzas 8-10

Those who watch him ride away grieve and lament their loss of him, saying that it's a pity to lose a lord who might one day have made such an excellent ruler. How much better, they say, that Gawain be made a ruler than that he be killed by an elf for overweening pride. And they complain against Arthur: "Who ever heard of a king who'd hear the counsel of drunken knights during Christmas games?" But Gawain rides on, traveling down many an unknown winding road. He rides through England ("Logres," a name originally suggesting sorrow), sleeps alone and friendless. He comes to Wales, passes Holy Head—a place where a saint was once (as Gawain expects to be) beheaded. He can find no one, among these grim and ungodly people, who has heard of the Green Chapel.

At last, abandoning roads, he plunges into the woods and searches on. The country he passes through now is gloomy and mysterious indeed. At every stream he meets some foe; he fights monsters, giants, evil men. But his worst foe of all is winter. Sleet falls, and he must sleep in his iron armor. At times he wakes up in the morning to find some huge waterfall-icicle hanging (like an ax) over his head. Thus he rides on in peril and misery, beset on all sides by at once horrible and comic reminder of the ax, until Christmas Eve. He prays to the Virgin that she reveal to him some resting place.

Stanzas 11-12

He is riding, as he prays, through a deep, ancient forest of *oak* trees where *hazel* and *hawthorn* (all plants associated with the ancient Druid religion and with Devil-worship, or witchcraft) are tangled thickly together, and birds pipe miserably for pain of the cold. He prays that he be shown some place where he may hear mass and Christmas matins, and he begins to sign the air with crosses on four sides. Just as he is signing the air the third time, he sees, as if miraculously, a great moated castle on a hill. He thanks Christ and St. Julian (patron saint of the traveler), and, giving his horse his head, comes entirely by chance to the chief gate. The bridge is suddenly raised, the gate bolted. "They feared no wind's blast," the poet comments.

Stanzas 13-14

Sir Gawain waits on the bank, looking at the castle. It is a splendid piece of architecture of the poet's own time, but many details make it seem mysterious, unreal. It is entirely white, its pinnacles seem numberless, it shimmers, and it looks like something cut out of clean, white paper. A porter comes to the wall and hails Sir Gawain. Gawain asks that the porter get permission from his lord to let him in. The porter agrees, leaves, and quickly returns with a great company, who let down the drawbridge and joyfully rush out to kneel in the snow, welcoming the stranger. Gawain is led into the central hall, where a great fire is burning on the hearth, and the lord of the castle warmly greets him.

There are suggestions everywhere in these two stanzas, particularly if one comes to them with the whole Pearl group in mind, that the castle in the oakwood, Hautdesert, is some sort of earthly paradise. It appears as if miraculously just when Gawain is praying for some worthy shelter; it is white, like the castle of the New Jerusalem as it is at some points described in *Pearl* (the idea of heaven as a white castle is very common in the Middle Ages); its splendid, artificial look recalls the castle-shaped ornaments in the Belshazzar section of *Purity*; and whereas Belshazzar's castle is described, with obvious allegorical intent, as "that rock," the description here contains some lines which, though not obviously allegorical, treat this rock castle in a way easily read as allegory:

> The rock went down in the water wonderfully deep,
> And above, it hove aloft to a huge height:
> Of hard-hewn stone it rose to the high tables
> Built up under the battlements, by the best law,
> And above stood splendid watch stations, evenly spaced....
> (lines 787-91)

The castle may be seen as an image of the cosmos, plunging deep into the sea, below, rising (virtually) to heaven, above. The tables (stone ledges reaching out to support the battlements) may be intended as a faint suggestion of tables of another sort, those supporting the celestial feast repeatedly mentioned in *Pearl* and *Purity*. That they are built "by the best law" is clear enough if on one level the law referred to is not architectural but divine.

However subtle and dubious these details may seem, punning and innuendo of this sort are common in the other poems. Recall the verbal play throughout *Pearl*, or the many subtle puns in *Purity*, for example the one at lines 607-08 which identifies the doom of Sodom and the Last Judgment: "If þay wer farande and fre and fayre to beholde,/ Hit is eþe to leve by þe last ende" — "If they were handsome and noble and fair to behold, it is easy to believe by what followed, *or* by the Last End."

The porter greets Gawain with "Yea, Peter" (i.e., Yes, by Peter), the name of heaven's keeper of the keys; and when the lord of the castle greets Gawain it is with the words, "All I have is yours to use at your will," an idea which, though natural enough on the literal level, obviously recalls God's generosity to the blessed in the New Jerusalem of *Pearl*. These suggestions continue in later stanzas, for instance in Gawain's change of clothes, analogous to the washing (transformation) of dress upon entering heaven in *Pearl*, and so forth, and in the symbolic appropriateness of the feast he is given.

All this is of course not to say that Hautdesert Castle is "really" heaven or a symbol of heaven. Neither the literal nor the allegorical level is all-important. The allegorical hints simply clarify what the castle is on the literal level: an earthly paradise of sorts, one which, like any earthly paradise (including Eden) can lead either to good or to bad, depending upon how men behave in it. A wrong step here can lead to a fall — and in fact the castle will lead Gawain to his fall from perfect virtue.

Stanzas 15-16

Gawain studies his host. Like the green man (though Gawain fails to make the connection), the host is huge, hearty, and mature. Like the green man, too, he wears a big beard and seems to glow with inner light, but this time all the imagery points not to the glow of green life but to a glow of cheerful fire. (Fire imagery is frequently mentioned here at Hautdesert.) The host's servants show Gawain to a splendid room and give him new clothes which make him look like Spring to the people around him, another detail supporting the death-regeneration theme in the poem. And again, as he did in his treatment of Camelot, the poet ironically points to apparent (but untested and here seemingly irrelevant) heroism: Sir Gawain looks like a prince without peer in the battlefield.

Then Gawain is brought to a table and given a feast, which the merry courtiers describe as his "penance." Their joke may be explained in a variety of ways, as simple irony (since the wealth of food suggests anything but grim penance), as an ironic reference to the fact that this meal, splendid as it is, is limited to fish, or as the poet's wry comment on the disparity between Gawain's temporary joy and vitality, on one hand, and his unchanged condition as a presumably condemned man, on the other.

Stanza 17

Delicately, the courtiers and the host put questions to Gawain to learn his identity. Discovering the truth, the lord is delighted, and all those around him say—with comic exaggeration that recalls the poet's description of Camelot's glory—that soon they will see splendid examples of courtly talk and fine manners. Though the lines have their inescapable comic side, they nevertheless recall the perfectly serious theme of "manners" as one reflection of purity in Pearl, Purity, and Patience. They suggest that the whole episode at Hautdesert Castle may prove a trial of Sir Gawain's purity of heart: everyone will be watching him, learning from him; and some, we learn very soon, will be tempting him as well.

Stanza 18

After his meal Sir Gawain goes to mass with his host and there meets the castle's two ladies, one as beautiful as a lady can be, the other as ugly as possible. Both are described, curiously enough, in images which suggest the apple, ancient symbol of Eden temptation. The younger lady shines in rich red and white, the older is yellow and black and has wrinkled skin. On the level of literal drama, the poet's device of presenting the two ladies together is superb craftsmanship, for each heightens the effect of the other: beauty is intensified by its foil and ugliness is intensified by beauty.

Stanzas 19-22

Gawain goes with the host and the ladies to a room with a large fireplace; servants bring beverages; and the host begins a Christmas game in which, piece by piece, he gives away his valuable clothes to those who win them by entertaining the company. At last Gawain retires.

The next day the company shares the Christmas feast, and the poet pauses to mention the seating arrangement. At the head of the table sits the old lady (Morgan le Fay, we learn later), a witch here occupying the same relative place the bishop occupied in Arthur's hall. Gawain sits next to the lady (wife of Bertilak, thus a lady known in some medieval legends as "the false Guinevere"), just as at Arthur's hall he sat next to the queen. And now the poet drops the first suggestion that something illicit is building up between the lady and Sir Gawain. They chatter — quite without hint of impropriety, the poet hastens to add — and while all the others at the feast mind their business, Gawain and the lady mind *theirs*.

In this way three pleasant days pass. At last it is time for the guests to leave and for Gawain to continue on his quest. He says good-bye to the host, who thanks him for his company and begs him to stay longer. Gawain refuses and at last explains the nature of his quest. Joyfully, the host tells him he knows the Green Chapel, which stands nearby. Gawain might easily remain at Hautdesert until New Year's day, then go out with a guide provided by the host and keep his appointment with the Green Knight.

Stanzas 23-24

Sir Gawain gladly accepts. They embrace and laugh, and then the host makes a proposal: since Gawain is tired from his long trip and from cavorting during the Christmas revels, he is to lie in bed late in the morning, resting up for his encounter, then keeping the host's wife company while the host rides out to hunt. The host adds one further stipulation. They will make a pact that whatever either may win in his adventures he will fully and truthfully exchange with the other. Gawain accepts, they talk a while longer, then all the company retires.

PART THREE

Stanzas 1-2

Before daylight the following morning the host and his huntsmen prepare for the hunt and set out after deer. The poet describes the day-long hunt in vivid detail, with a brilliant rush of rhythm and imagery — hunting horns "cracking as if all the cliffs had exploded" — and closes with an image of the energetic host leaping lightly again and again to and from his horse, driving the day to its close.

Stanzas 3-7

Then, leaving the hunt, the poet turns to Gawain's adventures in the castle. The knight awakens to find the lady stealthily entering his room. He peeks through the curtains at her and then, blushing, pretends to be asleep when she slips through the bed curtains and sits beside him. At last, seeing no other way out, he pretends to awaken and feigns surprise at finding her there. She flirts with him — boldly and fairly persuasively — pointing out that her lord is away on the hunt and all the castle is asleep, and threatens to close him in her arms. Gawain fends her off, comically polite; by midmorning the lady realizes that the knight may be impossible to seduce, since, for all her loveliness, his mind is on the grim stroke which awaits him at the Green Chapel. In the end she gets from him only a kiss. When she leaves, Gawain hastily dresses, and he spends the remainder of the day in polite, clever, and innocent dalliance with the young lady and the old one.

Stanzas 8-10

Returning to the deer hunt, the poet describes in detail the way in which the great kill is slaughtered and distributed among the hunters. Then all the company returns to the castle, where Gawain and the ladies are waiting. The host gives his catch to Gawain, who praises it as a better hunt than any he's seen "in the wintertime for seven years"—a courteous understatement. Gawain in turn gives his one prize to the host—the kiss. When the host asks where he got it, Gawain gracefully evades: that was not in the contract. They laugh and turn to the feast.

Stanzas 11-13

After the feast, the host and Gawain make the same contract for the following morning, each promising to exchange whatever he may win for the other's winnings: then they retire. At cockcrow the host leaps up with his men, and after a hasty mass and breakfast, they set off for the woods, this time in pursuit of boar. Again the poet describes the hunt in vivid and energetic detail. Gawain, meanwhile, lying in his bed, is again visited by the lady.

Stanzas 14-16

This time Gawain sits up boldly, directly greeting the lady. She playfully challenges him, arguing that he cannot be the virtuous Gawain, since he lacks manners. Gawain answers the challenge directly, saying—truthfully—that he cannot imagine what she means and asking to be told. He has forgotten to kiss her, the lady says. When Gawain answers that he failed to ask for fear he would be refused, the lady argues that he might have taken a kiss by force. Gawain dismisses that possibility as discourteous, and the lady takes another tack: she asks him to tell of his deeds of love and war. He answers that he will do so only if required to; otherwise it would be boasting. Again they get through the morning without transgression, Gawain dodging every effort of the temptress. From this meeting he gets two chaste kisses.

Stanzas 17-19

The boar hunt continues. The boar severely hurts dogs and men, but at last the host strikes the boar's deathblow and the dogs finish the job. Men and dogs cry out in triumph, the butchering begins, and at last the party turns homeward. At the castle, the host calls for Gawain, who quickly comes down.

Stanzas 20-22

Again the host and Gawain jokingly exchange gifts, the host getting, this time, the two kisses, and Gawain getting the boar. After the exchange they take dinner, and there the flirtatious lady presses Gawain so hard he is at times downright frightened. The host and Gawain agree on the same pact for the following day, then go to bed.

Stanzas 23-30

The host goes fox-hunting the following morning. The fox does all he can to trick his pursuers, but the host will not be shaken. Meanwhile, the lady of the castle gets up, dresses seductively, and goes to Gawain's room. She throws open Gawain's windows and calls out cheerfully to awaken him. Gawain mumbles in his gloomy sleep full of dreams of his forthcoming encounter with the Green Knight, then at last awakens and gazes with pleasure at the lady. They return to the flirtation eagerly, and Gawain is saved from a fall, the poet says, only by the Virgin's watchfulness.

The knight is sorely tempted, but he is checked by his concern, first, for his good name (an effect of loyal knightly service, or patience) and second, for what may happen if he betrays his obligation as a guest, that is, his manners, in the Pearl group identified with *purity*. The lady asks if he refuses her out of love for some other woman, and Gawain answers "by St. John" — an emblem of virginity — that he has pledged himself to no one (he is, of course, a servant of the Virgin — a virgin himself). The lady asks that he give her some gift she may remember him by, but Gawain slyly evades giving any token he cannot honestly give to another man's wife. Then the lady asks that he accept in any case a gift from her, and she shows him a splendid ring. Again he refuses, on the grounds that he cannot take a gift if he does not give one in return.

Now the lady offers him a sash which, though beautiful, is of slight worth in comparison to the ring and might be accepted without much shame. This too Gawain refuses. But when the lady tells him the sash has magical powers and can make the wearer invulnerable to any stroke, Gawain nervously reconsiders and at last accepts. The lady asks that he hide the gift from her lord, and Gawain agrees. In this day's encounter three kisses are exchanged.

The lady leaves, knowing she can get nothing more from the worthy man. Gawain gets up and goes to confession. He confesses in full, both major sins and minor. The poet says nothing of whether or not Gawain speaks of the sash to the priest, but it is clear that if he does repent of taking the sash he does not return it or change his purpose of wearing it to the Green Chapel. The rest of the day he spends with the company of the castle, and all who hear him remark that he was never more courteous than now. Then darkness comes.

Stanzas 31-34

The host meanwhile outwits and kills the fox, and the company returns to the castle. This time, nervously perhaps, Gawain asks to give his gift first, and he gives the host the three kisses he has won, saying nothing of the sash. The host with wry jokes, including an allusion to St. Giles (who was beheaded), gives the fox to Sir Gawain and tells the story of its capture.

Then they all eat, laughing and joking. When the time comes for going to bed, Gawain thanks the host for all his kindness and asks that the host remember his promise to provide him a guide to the Green Chapel. The host says he will do so, paying all he may ever have promised in full. Mournfully then Gawain goes to bed, where it may be (the poet cannot say) he has distressing dreams, for his sad quest is near its end.

Throughout Gawain's stay at Hautdesert Castle, the audience is meant to understand, there is more going on than meets the eye. As discussions by Savage and Utley show (see Bibliography), there are subtle relationships between the host's hunts and the lady's three temptations. While the host hunts deer, Gawain, hunted by the lady, reacts rather like a deer, first lying still in hopes of escaping the huntress, then nimbly evading her pursuit by heightened alertness. While the host hunts boar, Gawain reacts to the lady's temptation in direct and frontal, boarlike fashion. And while the host hunts the fox, Gawain responds to the lady's temptation with cunning, arguing against her offers of gifts by sophistry and at last accepting one of her gifts because of his foxy hope of outwitting the Green Knight.

The hunts have also another level of significance. Deer are hunted for food; boar prove the courage or mettle of the hunter; the fox proves the hunter's wit. The three animals may thus be seen as emblematic of the three souls of man—that is, the concupiscent soul, or desiring faculty; the irascible soul which gives man courage, steadfast loyalty, and rightful or wrongful wrath; and the intellectual faculty.

The lady's first temptation is bluntly sexual. At one point, in fact, the lady boldly offers her body for Gawain to use as he may please. In her second temptation, mainly a temptation of Gawain's "irascible soul," the lady first suggests that Gawain seize a kiss by force, then urges him to boast of his conquests, both of which would be unhealthy activities of the irascible soul. In the final temptation the lady attempts a perversion of right reason in Gawain—that he make himself her servant rather than the Virgin's, that he accept a ring, figurative of worldly pride, and finally that he seek to preserve his life by his own means rather than through faith in God or, more specifically, through the purity of his own heart and patience, or loyal devotion, to the larger order. The last temptation is successful; Gawain will leave Hautdesert Castle less perfect than he was when he came. A similar emphasis on the tripartite soul informs *Pearl* (cf. the "three errors," lines 291 ff.).

PART FOUR

Stanzas 1-4

New Year's Day arrives, a day of winter sleet described in terms which recall the poet's earlier comments on the changing seasons and which thus remind the audience of the earlier theme of natural and inevitable change in the birth-death-regeneration cycle; but for Gawain there seems no hope for regeneration here in this world. The time of respite is over. The knight lies in bed listening to the storm and then, before dawn, he gets up, lights a lamp, and calls his chamberlain.

His clothes and armor are brought to him, and he finds that all his equipment is polished and rubbed free of rust. In the light of earlier passages in the Pearl group, the detail has significant overtones. The armor *was* rusty but is now rubbed free, just as, in *Purity*, the pearl that was stained by use in the world can be cleaned again or just as, in *Pearl*, dress made dirty in the world can be made radiant. There is still a chance for Gawain, these details hint. If one cannot be saved by purity (and he is, after all, very close at least to his original purity), he can be saved by repolishing of the kind described in *Purity*, true confession.

Gawain arms himself, becoming, in the poet's words, the handsomest man from here to Greece — a phrase which echoes the poet's description of the jeweler's happiness, in *Pearl*, when he discovers his child. Gawain does not forget the sash, but if his motivation is imperfect, he is partly excused by the poet: Gawain does not wear the sash for its beauty or value but to save his life.

The sash is, as Professor Howard has pointed out, the second of the poem's two pivotal symbols. Whereas the shield symbolizes Gawain's proper outer and inner nature, the sash symbolizes his fall. It represents worldliness (the medieval sash or belt is used to carry money bags, keys, and the like), and it probably also represents secrecy, Gawain's loss of that openness and courtesy which formerly distinguished him. But Gawain's worldliness, the poet insists, is tempered: he is not proud in the sense that he craves worldly glory but only in the sense that, valuing his own life above all other things, he forgets his higher nature.

On the day Christ first shed blood (in circumcision, for the Middle Ages a foreshadowing of his death), Gawain mounts his horse, bids farewell to his host and all the company, and starts on his way with the guide the host has provided. They ride through a gloomy landscape of mists, steep mountain walls, broiling waterways, and stones shattered by their fall from the high cliffs (as Gawain too may be broken). At the crown of a high hill the servant pauses and stops Sir Gawain.

Stanzas 5-7

Now Gawain suffers another temptation. The guide tells him terrible stories of the cruelty of the green man dwelling in the Green Chapel and begs him not to go on. The guide will tell no one of the cowardice, he promises: for love of Gawain he cannot watch him willingly go to his death. Gawain is revolted by the plea, but he rejects it with grudging courtesy. The guide gives the knight his helmet and spear, declares that he would not go a step farther for anything, and turns back.

Critics have sometimes supposed that the guide is the shape-shifting host himself in yet another disguise. The point cannot be proved one way or the other, and admittedly the text raises problems in this regard. On one hand, it does seem un- likely that the host would bring a servant into his plot (as one critic argues); on the other hand, it seems odd that anyone not in on the plot could seriously speak of a green man who has murdered people for years and years, since the green man, we learn later, was created by Morgan on this occasion to trouble Arthur's court.

Nevertheless, both the host and the guide are apparently present at the time Gawain leaves Hautdesert. And the guide's temptation seems not demonic or calculated but human and ingenuous. From all indications he acts from misguided love of Gawain, begging him to abandon the quest because the loss of so noble a life would be a great waste. (Compare the feelings of Arthur's court when Gawain leaves.) As a man of low station, the guide has no great concern for honor. Gawain, showing that he *does* care for honor, demonstrates that, though he may have lost some of his purity, he has not lost his knightly loyalty or "patience." The tone of his words to himself after the churl has left shows that he does indeed act with true patience, accepting God's will, and trusting only a little, if at all, to the magic in the sash he wears.

Stanzas 8-11

Gawain rides down into the valley floor the guide has pointed out and, looking around, sees no sign of any ordinary chapel. What he sees, instead, is an ancient barrow, clearly no Christian chapel but, as he imagines, a thing of the Devil. The Green Knight is nowhere near, it seems. Then Gawain hears the honing of a terrible ax. Gawain calls out, announcing that he has come as promised, and a voice calls back from high in the cliffs telling him to wait. At last, charging out of a hole in a rock —exactly as the boar did earlier—the Green Knight comes to him. Rather than wading the stream, he vaults in on his ax, as would a witch that cannot touch water. Gawain bows cautiously —he is dreadfully conscious that he may soon be beheaded—and the green man praises him for keeping his word. Gawain bends over for the stroke he has promised to accept.

Stanzas 12-17

The Green Knight raises his ax and brings it down but at the last minute stops himself, for Gawain has flinched. The Green Knight mocks Sir Gawain for his apparent cowardice, saying "*I* didn't flinch like that." Gawain answers angrily that he will not shy again but adds that there is a difference between their two situations: if *his* head falls he will not be able to pick it up again. Then he urges the Green Knight to act quickly. The Green Knight lifts his ax to strike again, but again withholds the blow. He cheerfully praises Gawain for not flinching this time. Gawain furiously demands that the green man strike and get it over with. The green man mocks his wrath but agrees and lifts the ax again. This time he strikes just hard enough to cut the skin, then checks the blow. The instant Gawain sees drops of blood in the snow, he leaps back, throwing his shield into place, and stands ready now to defend himself, for he has fulfilled his bargain and need not take another stroke without defense.

The huge green man stands idly leaning on the sharp blade of his ax and admires Gawain's brave though slightly ludicrous stance. Then laughingly he tells Gawain to relax and explains that he has purposely spared him. The two harmless strokes were payment for Gawain's complete faith during the first two exchanges at Hautdesert Castle; the tap which cut Gawain's neck is payment for the slight fault on Gawain's part in the third exchange. The green man, host of Hautdesert Castle, prompted his wife's temptations himself; the sash Gawain accepted was the host's property. Nevertheless, the Green Knight says, Gawain is as faithful a man as he has ever seen on earth.

Gawain is astounded; then he weeps at his disgrace. He declares himself guilty of cowardice and covetousness — cowardice in the face of death, covetousness toward his own life — and he hurls the sash at its owner. But the Green Knight laughs, dismissing Gawain's grief and shame. He tells Gawain that he now holds him guiltless, since Gawain is cleanly confessed and bears the obvious penance of the wound on his neck. Like the repolished armor, or like the pearl renewed in wine (in *Purity*), Gawain is now, from the Green Knight's point of view, as innocent as on the day he was born. (The allusion to confession as polishing, in *Purity*, is explicit. The Green Knight calls Gawain "polished of that plight [fault] and purified...clean.") He gives the sash to Gawain as a gift and asks him to return with him to Hautdesert, promising no more harm will come to him there.

Stanzas 18-20

Gawain refuses the invitation, partly from shame, no doubt, but also, explictly, from a sense that he has been over-worldly in reveling with the host. He should not be surprised, he says, at having been tricked by a woman, for many others have been tricked—Adam, Solomon, Samson, David. The lines obviously express Gawain's anger at the temptress, but they perhaps have also a more general implication. From the standard medieval point of view, any decline from reason to passion is a decline from the masculine (symbolized, for instance, by Adam) to the feminine (symbolized, for instance, by Eve). He agrees, however, to keep the sash, saying he will use it as a sign of his shame and will wear it wherever he goes to remind himself of humility. Then he asks the Green Knight's name and learns that he is Bertilak (traditional husband of the false, or counterfeit, Guine-vere) and that the whole scheme was arranged by Morgan le Fay, the old woman in the castle, who through hatred of Guinevere sought to frighten her to death by sending the green man to Camelot. He again invites Gawain to come home with him, and again Gawain politely refuses.

Stanzas 21-22

Gawain turns home, fighting his way past enemies, as he was forced to do when he came. The scar heals and he wears the sash over it like a baldric. He comes to the court and is joyfully received. He tells his story, including the story of his disgrace, and he tells the court that the baldric is the sign of his shame. The court laughs and tries to comfort him, for he did, after all, come off much better than most men would have done. And since he refuses ever to remove the baldric, the king and all the court cheerfully agree that they too will wear a green baldric, not so much as a sign of their share in Gawain's disgrace as a sign of honor to the great Sir Gawain.

All these things, the poet concludes, took place in the time of Arthur's reign, after the fall of Troy. May He who bore the crown of thorns bring all men to bliss!

Gawain, it should be observed, is renewed in two ways at the end of the poem, religiously, through the confession, or mock-confession, given by the Green Knight, and socially, through the court's acceptance of the baldric as a sign of honor. He has been tested, as every mortal is tested and, like every mortal with the exception of Christ (who was also tested in the wilderness in three ways, for right reason, right passion, and right desire), Gawain did not completely pass the test. But faults can be forgiven, and harms can be undone. After winter, as the poet reminds us throughout, comes spring, and after a fall, redemption. The poet's opening and closing focus on Troy reminds the audience that civilizations, too, fall and rise again. And his focus in this poem on the Christmas season reminds his listeners of the greatest of all renewals in the Christian scheme, the fall of mankind undone by Christ in a bargain ironically opposite to the Green Knight's bargain—a life for a life.

Review Questions

1. Closely analyze the structure of *Pearl*. Obviously many passages in the poem are borrowed (the Parable of the Vineyard, the vision of the New Jerusalem, etc.); other passages are apparently original. A modern poet – Ezra Pound, for example – might also build a poem largely out of quotations, but he would be likely to make a rather different use of the quotations. What is the function of the familiar material in *Pearl?* To what extent do the borrowed materials have a meaning or esthetic value in *Pearl* which they do not have outside it? To put this another way, has the poet transmuted his borrowed material, has he interpreted it by placing it in a new context, has he simply borrowed it for its pleasantly familiar ring, or what? To what extent do the original and borrowed passages comment upon one another, developing a unified vision?

2. *Pearl* presents a curious blend of personal observation and accepted opinion or dogma. Point out specific instances of the poet's use of closely observed life – Nature, people, events – and instances of his use of dogmatic or conventional opinion. To what extent does each way of thinking support or oppose the other? Is the poem best described as a personal elegy by a bereaved father or as a versified sermon? If it seems to you to be both, are the elegiac and homelitic strains harmonized and ultimately resolved? Explain.

3. Trace the development of the following images in the poem: the pearl, the jeweler, the garden, the well, music. Critics have identified the pearl in a variety of ways (as a symbol of the Virgin Mary, as a symbol of the eucharistic wafer, and so on). In the light of your tracing of the image in all its permutations, comment on any core of meaning you can find in the image.

4. Throughout *Pearl* there are instances of transmuted Nature —the rose which turns into a gem, for example. Collect as many cases of such transmutation as you can find and comment on the significance of this motif. The poem itself, as we said earlier, is a ring or "garland" of one hundred and one stanzas (perhaps viewed in the poet's own time as a ring of twelve-line sonnets). To what extent does the form of the poem support the poem's theme?

5. Note the verbal repetitions which link stanzas in each of the five-stanza blocks. Do the repeated words and phrases have particular significance; in other words, are they in any way crucial to the meaning or effect of the passages in which they occur? The fifteenth section has six stanzas instead of five. Assuming that this is no error—though critics have argued it may be—why has the poet chosen the fifteenth section instead of some other? Why does he write one hundred and one stanzas instead of, say, a neat one hundred? (Is there any *direct* meaningful relationship between this choice and the poet's choice, in *Sir Gawain and the Green Knight,* of the time span of a year and a day?) What other number symbolism does the poem contain—in specific references, in the form of the stanza chosen, or elsewhere?

6. In what ways is *Pearl* a dissatisfying poem? To what extent are its limitations, if it has any, effects of its medievalness?

7. To what extent does the poet appear to show the direct influence of Dante? What details, techniques, or ideas in *Pearl* invite comparison with things found in Chaucer's *Book of the Duchess?*

8. In *Sir Gawain and the Green Knight* the poet calls much less attention to artificial form than he does in *Pearl.* Is there significance in the fact that *Sir Gawain* is in four parts? Do form and content interpenetrate, in this poem, in other ways as well? Is it possible to argue that the manuscript's illuminated capitals point up significant formal breaks in the story? (See Howard's description of the manuscript.)

9. Camelot is clearly a civilized court, in effect the product of a civilized though troubled line going back to ancient Troy. Hautdesert Castle, on the other hand, is located in uncharted wilderness. What is the point of this contrast? What features do Camelot and Hautdesert have in common? What are the chief differences between the two courts? Civilization is one of Gawain's defenses against evil. In what ways is this shown? To what extent is the defense effective? Can it be shown that civilization is at the same time spiritually dangerous? (Gawain says, in leaving Bertilak, that he has reveled too much already. Is he speaking merely from momentary shame, or does the poet perhaps take a dim view of courtly revels? How, then, can one account for the poet's obvious delight in splendid dress, furniture, feasts, and the like?)

10. The Green Knight is vividly and realistically characterized, yet he seems to be, at the same time, a symbol, and a rather confusing one. On one hand the poet explains him as an illusion created by the magician Morgan le Fay; on the other hand, Gawain's guide claims the green man has occupied the barrow for a long, long time, and when the green man rides away the poet hints, strangely, that he does not know where the green man goes. There is a similar confusion, as Larry Benson points out, in the poet's description of the green man. He is like a beautiful elf (of the old, large sort), on one hand; on the other hand he is like the conventional wild man of medieval tales. The castle he occupies is equally mysterious. Is all this obscurity purposeful both dramatically and symbolically? What does the green man appear to represent? What details in the poem tend to identify him with the Devil? with witchcraft? with some northern pagan god? with Cupid? Can he be understood as a mythic personification of Nature itself?

11. Like *Pearl, Sir Gawain and the Green Knight* makes use of sources. (See Benson's study, Selected Bibliography.) Compare the poet's use of sources here with his use of sources in *Pearl*. To what extent is the very different use of sources in the two works an effect of some difference in purpose?

12. Discuss the treatment of women in *Sir Gawain and the Green Knight*, commenting not only on the ladies of Hautdesert and the temptresses Gawain castigates near the end of the poem but also on Guinevere and the Virgin. What did poor Guinevere ever do to Morgan to make the old witch want to kill her?

13. Discuss *Sir Gawain and the Green Knight* as a psychological novel. Can it be read, also, as satire? as romantic comedy? Comment in detail on ways in which the poem's effects alter when the poem is *not* read in the context of the whole Pearl group, that is, as a conclusion following *Pearl, Purity,* and *Patience.*

Selected Bibliography

Texts

The Complete Works of the Gawain-Poet, trans. JOHN GARDNER. Chicago, 1965. Good introduction, but mistakenly attributes *St. Erkenwald* to the poet. Translation vivid but rather free; it is the only translation that maintains the rhythm and the symbolic structure of the poems.

Cleanness, ed. SIR ISRAEL GOLLANCZ. London, 1921. Contains useful but outdated notes.

Pearl, ed. E. V. GORDON. Oxford, 1953. Includes notes on lines, comments on authorship, dialect, manuscript, etc.

Pearl and Sir Gawain and the Green Knight, ed. A. C. CAWLEY. London and New York, 1962. Classroom edition with foot-note translation and commentary.

Purity, ed. R. J. MENNER. New Haven, 1920. Good discussion of alliterative technique, comments on authorship, etc.

Sir Gawain and the Green Knight, ed. SIR ISRAEL GOLLANCZ. London, 1940. Superb edition; excellent introduction and notes.

Sir Gawain and the Green Knight, ed. J. R. R. TOLKIEN and E. V. GORDON. London, 1930. Valuable supplement to Gollancz; excellent notes.

Criticism

BENSON, LARRY. *Art and Tradition in Sir Gawain and the Green Knight.* New Brunswick, N.J., 1965. Excellent on direct sources. Thesis on Gawain's traditional guilt as informing the present poem very doubtful. Good on style.

BORROFF, MARIE. *Sir Gawain and the Green Knight: A Stylistic and Metrical Study.* New Haven, 1962. Excellent on style and humor; weak on rhythm.

EAGEN, JOSEPH F. "The Import of Color Symbolism in *Sir Gawain and the Green Knight,*" *St. Louis University Studies.* n.d. Highly speculative.

FLETCHER, JEFFERSON B. "The Allegory of the Pearl," *JEGP,* XX (1921), 1-21. Inferior to Wellek's analysis (below).

HOWARD, DONALD R. "Structure and Symmetry in *Sir Gawain,*" *Speculum,* XXXIX (1964), 425-33. One of the best available studies. Generally supports the more elaborate reading of Benson.

MADELEVA, SISTER M. *Pearl: A Study in Spiritual Dryness.* New York, 1925. Very narrow interpretation, but interesting.

SAVAGE, HENRY. *The Gawain-Poet: Studies in His Personality and Background.* Chapel Hill, 1956. Opening discussion very useful.

SCHOFIELD, W. H. "The Nature and Fabric of the Pearl," *PMLA,* XIX (1904), 154-215. Inferior to Wellek's study.

SPEIRS, JOHN. *Medieval English Poetry: The Non-Chaucerian Tradition.* London, 1957. Highly original, highly speculative; not well received by critics.

UTLEY, F. L. "Folklore, Myth, and Ritual," *Critical Approaches to Medieval Literature,* ed. DOROTHY BETHURUM. New York, 1960.

WELLEK, RENÉ. "The Pearl: An Interpretation of the Middle-English Poem," *Studies in English,* IV (Prague, 1933), 17 ff. The best study, with valuable summary of earlier opinion.

NOTES

NOTES